A Straig[illegible] Living and Working Abroad

How to live and work — anywhere in the world

by Jonathan Packer

Straightforward Publishing

www.straightforwardco.co.uk

Living and Working Abroad

Jonathan Packer is a writer, journalist and editor whose other books include *Live and Work in Russia and Eastern Europe*, *Live and Work in Spain and Portugal*, and *The Directory of Jobs and Careers Abroad;* and a contributor to publications like *The Times* and *Overseas Jobs Express* on such subjects as living and working abroad, travel, and education.

He has lived and worked abroad himself; and has a keen interest in travel and life in other countries — and been *"everything from an English teacher to a film extra,"* he says — and lives in Oxford, UK.

Jonathan Packer

A Straightforward Guide to *Living and Working Abroad*

How to live and work — anywhere in the world

Published by Straightforward Publishing, 38 Cromwell Road, London E17 9JN, UK

The editorial of this book was completed in April 2000

ISBN 1899924 78 7

Printed by Polestar Wheatons Ltd, Exeter

Cover design by Straightforward Graphics

Typesetting by SEI, PO Box 126, Oxford OX2 6UB, UK

While every effort has been taken to ensure that the information in this book is accurate at the time of going to print, the author and the publisher cannot accept liability for any errors or omissions, or changes in the law

Straightforward Publishing

www.straightforwardco.co.uk

"When I came to reflect, what a change!"

— William Cobbett

Introduction

Accountancy in Afghanistan? Zookeeping in Zimbabwe? This book won't tell you how to do this! But it will tell you more about where to go, what to do, how to get there and 'how to live and work anywhere in the world.'

If you are going there for work or business — in the summer or for retirement — or you are looking to get a job on the spot — *A Straightforward Guide to Living and Working Abroad* can help. It covers all the various stages of going to live and work in another country; and tells you about living there short or long term; not just as a tourist.

There are five chapters, which cover the main stages of your transition abroad. And there are sections in each of these chapters — on *Working abroad, Getting a job, Getting there, Settling in and Living abroad* — which will give you some more background information and suggestions for contacts you can make yourself, like embassies and tourist offices.

Appendix 1 is a list of *Direct Contacts,* giving some other directions you could take; and *Appendix 2* contains a variety of different *Sources of Information. Appendix 3* has some *Personal Experiences* of living abroad, with some ideas you could follow up. These are people who have lived and worked abroad before.

You can look at the different sections in the chapters which interest you — like the 'A – Z of jobs abroad' in Chapter 1 — or the different ways suggested of getting a job abroad in Chapter 2 — and then the appendix / personal experience sections for more names and addresses, ideas and contacts.

You could find out everything from travel trade fairs to how to get to Tristan da Cunha . . . The *Index* is where you can go to find any country or organization — to find out where a particular country or the main subjects in these chapters are mentioned. There are some interesting *Websites* at the end.

There are also links or references between sections — and information to follow up — with a summary of the *Key Points* at the end — to make this book as simple and practical to use as possible.

The main idea was to write a book you can read, and enjoy reading. And to give the right background to living and working abroad. And a useful one too — which you can use to help you make this move to a different country successfully — unlike the character played by Leonardo DiCaprio in the recent film 'The Beach' — and avoid some of his mistakes . . . It is about gaining new experiences, and learning from experience.

This will help you go through each of these stages — of 'Working abroad','Getting a job', Getting there', 'Settling in', and 'Living abroad' — at least more successfully than he did!

Some will be moving more or less for good. Others will go for a short time, for a summer job or in their 'gap' year, or on a posting there. Many probems will be practical, which will affect almost everyone, like buying a ticket or getting a visa. And there are all the more difficult-to-define questions, like the effect on children and family life; or what it will be like to live in a different country.

This is what this book is about. It has all the contacts you need to find out more. And ideas for all kinds of jobs, whether you are going to Belgium or Borneo, Jamaica or Japan.

This is a new kind of guide. You are welcome to make your own contribution in the future — from anywhere in the world — there is a *Questionnaire* for this at the end of Chapter 5 — and to send in your comments for future editions.

And it also tells a story: of anyone going to work, and travel and live abroad. Is this you?

Jonathan Packer

Oxford, April 2000

Acknowledgements

Books need a 'thank you', and as the writer Umberto Eco says, "*skill in making acknowledgements is the hallmark of the thorough-bred scholar.*" I would like to disclaim any such knowledge, and thank Straightforward Publishing for commissioning this book, and my wife Reiko Packer for her help, support and kindness.

Contents

1

Working abroad

"There are literally hundreds of ideas you can follow up — and jobs you can do. The person it depends on is you"

Who, what, where, when 1.1

You should think of who you are, where you want to go, and when to make a start. What kind of job do you want to do?

Even if you are moving in a year or two, the time to start is now

And why 1.2

This is not a question you can always answer easily before you get there. But you should think about this too — to clarify your aims and objectives.

For example, it might be that you have decided to go because you wanted to go to a certain country. Or to continue your career. Or you might have been sent there by your company or organization.

And some people go to live and work abroad because maybe they have married someone from that country. Others have been on vacation there before — and then decided to stay. Some study; and others might go for a year or two, to work and travel. It all depends on you.

You might be going alone; or travelling with friends or family. And some will go to enjoy a quiet life away from it all, in a warmer climate, somewhere they like the way of life . . .

And everyone really has more complicated reasons than this for wishing to live and work in another country. A little reflection and on who you are and where you are going in life will help to start

Help and support 1.3

First of all you should think of all the possible sources of help you have and support, which you will need for such a big change. Even if you are relying on your own resources, you should consider other people. If you get into trouble, who can help?

You are moving your whole life as well as your work to a new location. This is not something you can do without some back-up — as well as the motivation to do this — which comes from you

Five stages of living and working abroad 1.4

If you are thinking there is too much to do, and too many things to sort out before departure, you can think about it in five different stages: *Working abroad*, *Getting a job*, *Getting there*, *Settling in*, and *Living abroad*.

These are the chapters in this book, where you can find out more about these different stages — and look at these one by one

Who can get a job abroad? 1.5

Almost everyone *can* go. The choice is not so simple though. At least as many will go from the poorer countries to the rich ones as the other way — to make a better life for themselves. But this is a different way of looking at life — not as a matter of choice but because you have to.

Here, your motivation may be to survive and get by, not just to get on and make a career.

These are the two main types of emigration and immigration in the world. As The Beatles *said, 'money can't buy you love' — but without enough money you can't find many of the other necessities of life either; and this is one reason why many people — from countries rich and poor — go to live and work abroad*

An A - Z of jobs abroad 1.6

Here are some of the possible jobs you could do. But remember this book is about you finding your own answers to these questions. Going to live and work abroad will be the beginning of your own story, and not exactly like any of the examples suggested here.

Agriculture. *International Agricultural Exchanges* (tel UK 0800-783-2186; e-mail uk@agriventure.com; *www.agriventure.com*). *"We'll put the world at your feet," Australia, Canada, New Zealand, USA, Japan* . . . Not cane-cutting on some *Thai* island . . . In the *UK*, there is 'Farmers Weekly;' and *www.agriculture.com*

Building work — see 'The builders,' *Personal Experiences*

Cultural organizations. These organizations and institutes — which you can find in — and sometimes outside — the major cities — can be a good source for jobs directly, not only in the cultural area, but for secretaries, tutors, language teachers, administrators, and drivers, gardeners, cooks . . . and a source of more information about the country too:

The *British Council* can supply a list of their offices and libraries / resource centres around the world. Their (often busy) information line is UK 0161-957 7755; fax 0161-957 7762; e-mail general.enquiries@britcoun.org

Committee for the Advancement of Arab-British Understanding (CAABU), Arab British Centre, 21 Collingham Road, London SW5, UK; tel 0207-373 8414; fax 0207-835 2058; e-mail caabu@arab-british.u-net.com

Daiwa Anglo-Japanese Foundation, 13-14 Cornwall Terrace, London NW1 4QP, UK; tel 0207-486 2914

Dante Alighieri Society, 18 Hans Court, Hans Road, London SW3 1RX, UK; tel 0207-823 8955 — offers language courses and cultural events — for *Italy* — with other centres around the world

Finnish Institute, 35-36 Eagle Street, 38 Chesham Place, London WC1R 4AJ; tel 0207-404 3309; fax 0207-404 8893; is an educational, cultural and artistic centre with a library with useful research materials

The *Hispanic and Luso Brazilian Council*, Canning House, 2 Belgrave Square, London SW1X 8PJ, UK; tel 0207-235 2303; fax 0207-235 3587 — has a library of interest to anyone wishing to know more about the Portuguese/Spanish-speaking world. For a small fee their 'Education Department' will send you lists of contacts for international travellers and people going to *Spain*, *Portugal*, or Latin America to study, or live and work. And this is a centre for expatriate organizations like the *Anglo Portuguese Society* and others for the Latin American countries — e.g. the *British–Uraguayan Society* — and Portuguese-speaking Africa.

The *Institute of Latin American Studies*, 31-35 Tavistock Square, London SW1Y 8PJ, UK; tel 0207-387 5671; fax 0207-388 5024

Swedish Embassy Cultural Section, UK: tel 0207-724 2101

United States Information Service, 24 Grosvenor Square, London W1X 9LS, UK; tel 0207-499 9000

And similar organizations where you are. Many countries would also have a 'cultural section,' *or* 'cultural counsellor,' *at their embassy — see* Embassies and Consulates 1.18 *below. Their library or 'resource centre' is often a good place to write to*

Design — see 'The designer,' *Personal Experiences*

Engineering. *Overseas Jobs Express* is a good source of engineering and technical jobs: Premier House, Shoreham Airport, Sussex BN43 5FF, UK; tel 01273-440220; fax 01273-440229; e-mail editor@overseasjobs.com; *www.overseasjobs.com.*

And see the *Direct Contacts* section in this book too

English teaching. See 'St. Giles Language Teaching Center' and 'CLIC IH' in *Direct Contacts* — and under 'Teaching' below; *www.stgiles-usa.com* and *www.clic.es.* For more about English teaching and where this may lead see *Personal Experiences* p.207

Farming. See 'Agriculture.' Also 'At home abroad' in *Personal Experiences*

Gardens. *Garden tours* — leading a group of people on a specialized holiday. This means first of all you will need a strong interest in the subject — and the country. You could get a job in your own — or for any holiday guiding or group leader job for which this also applies. 'Tour operators' are where you could look in the phone book (travel agencies do a different thing, they sell tickets). Or under 'Schools and universities,' or 'Education,' for educational tours — and if you have an interest in the country, or its culture, or travel, or teaching you could follow this route. *Garden centres* are where you might find a job — see *Shops* below. *Garden design.* You need an interest in the subject first, then to make some new contacts

Health work — see 'The health worker,' *Personal Experiences*

The Internet — and how to use it. You could end up literally anywhere. But this is virtual reality, not anywhere necessarily you would want to go. A search on the garden theme led me from flowers, to florists, to a florist — by using the *American Yellow Pages* at *www.athand.com,* which really means this is close at hand. It led me to a choice, of state, city name . . . then to the *68th Street Florist,* 403 E 68th St., New York, NY 10021-6305, tel 212-737-9700, *USA,* with a map, directions, and even details for 'What's nearby' to help you get there

Journalism — see 'Journalism,' *Personal Experiences*

K-FOR / French Foreign Legion. Join the army, of any country which is part of the United Nations, and your job is likely to be international. Gurkhas — from *Nepal* — are currently serving with the British contingent of K-FOR, for instance, the UN peacekeeping force in *Kosovo.* And police services are becoming more international too. The French Foreign Legion take not just anyone, or is it just anybody? I can never quite remember. The correct procedure for this is to go to your local *gendarmerie* — in *France,* or in any of its *DOM-TOM* or overseas territories from *Martinique* to *New Caledonia;* and they will tell where the nearest recruiting place is. One *séjour* — or posting — abroad is guaranteed for every five years of service

L for *LIBA* — see below

Merchant or investment banking. *London Investment Banking Association (LIBA),* 6 Frederick's Place, London EC2R 8BT, UK. They started as merchants, and providers of financial services; and became international investment banks, *"often represented overseas"*

Never be too programmatic about these things. You don't need to fill in all the spaces . . . Just do the right things which you think will get you a job. Use your creativity. You can find the *UK Yellow Pages* at *www.yell.co.uk,* for instance, but also — probably — somewhere in a library near you.

Where 'N' would take you to 'Nanny and Childcare agencies,' and many which deal with jobs around the world

Open University. The *Open University* can be for study almost anywhere, at diploma or university level — the modules add up to the equivalent of a degree. They see themselves as a European and worldwide organization, not just a British one.

Contact: The Open University, PO Box 625, Milton Keynes MK7 6AA, UK; hotline: 0870-9000 301; international line 01908-653744; *www.open.ac.uk/brochure*. Or, for jobs, write to the OU at Walton Hall, Milton Keynes MK7 6AA, UK; tel 01908-274066; fax 01908-653744 — *"altogether a better place to work."*

Or *www.open.ac.uk/employment*; or *www-tec.open.ac.uk*; or *www.jobs.ac.uk*

The OU has a 'recruitment hotline': tel 01908-654161 or 655062 or 654144; or contact the individual department which can point you in the right direction.

They also employ tutors around the world

Packer. I looked up my name on the internet — it seemed to be the moment to do it — and found — when I went to *www.summerjobs.com* — a job for a 'Packing Barn Supervisor' in Ontario, Canada — for a 'hands-on packer.' This would be from "*Sweet Cherries in June / July to Pears in the Fall;*" and is a "*job for the year 2000*" it says.

Surnames can often be the names of jobs — or places where people have lived and worked in the past — or are named for a certain place or profession. They often record a movement from one place to another for work or travel if you think about it.

The third main category of surnames is for people — and this applies in almost any language . . . names also show how living and working in another place is a universal part of all our histories.

'Packer' refers to the days — in England — when packhorses would carry goods like wool down to a market or port, from where they might be sent on or exported to almost anywhere in the world.

I just thought you might like to know . . . and see 4.14 on language and languages

Questionnaire. There is a questionnaire in this book you can fill in, at the end of the chapter on *Living Abroad,* which you are welcome to photocopy and return — to PO Box 126, Oxford OX2 6UB, UK — along with any comments you may have

All contributions, personal experiences, and ideas for future books are very welcome

Retirement. Which doesn't always mean not working, but often retired people continue with a part-time job, or something they enjoy doing, wherever they are living. And this is one tip for enjoying a successful retirement abroad.

A very good guide for older women, especially, travelling abroad is *The world at your feet* by Nina Hathway, published by *Age Concern England*, 1268 London Road, London SW16 4ER, UK. It covers meeting people and travelling independently.

"*One of the bonuses of getting older,*" she says, "*is that there is more time to explore the world . . . whether it is now because you can enjoy the luxury of retirement or simply have more time to spend now that career and family are no longer so all consuming.*"

Age Concern also publishes factsheets for travel for older people

Shops. You don't always need to speak the language fluently to work in shops — dealing with the public — but you do need to speak some. Then there are all the jobs behind the scenes, from warehouse work to distribution . . . and some international stores offering a career structure for their managers which may take them abroad. Mentioned above, *Age Concern* also runs charity shops; and this is a very good way to do volunteer or intern work in many countries — by working as a volunteer in one of these. Probably better not to contact head office, but go in and ask, or write to the local one — addressed to 'The Manager.'

This is the best way, generally speaking, to approach smaller shops, bars, restaurants on the high street — and we have seen how you might find a name and address through the internet, and there are phone books, recruitment agencies . . . And best of all, for anything from hairdressing to hotel work — and for many other places like these — is just to go in and ask.

Especially where there is quite low unemployment — or at the height of the tourist season — these jobs will be easy to find. Or work in a **souvenir shop** — where speaking your own language might be an advantage . . . You can look for work on the spot

Teaching. Jeff Ely, Personnel Recruitment, *AEON Corp.*, 250 Park Avenue, Suite 1000, New York, NY 10169, USA — for teaching English in *Japan*

Universities. These have schools, departments, and libraries which recruit staff with the right language abilities and interests, for example the *School of Oriental and African Studies (SOAS)* at the *University of London* — their *Japan Research Centre* being an example of this kind of academic organization: tel 0207-637 2388.

To find out more about any country, you may find there are lectures and interest group meetings — like the *Japan Interest Group*, School of Social Sciences, *Brookes University*, Oxford OX3 0BP, UK. *And see under 'Open University' previously*

Voluntary work. *The Prince's Trust* is headed by Prince Charles. It offers disadvantaged young people week-away courses in the *UK* — and grants for them to start off in business — also a *Go and See* grant which will pay for a ticket and some expenses to go and see how volunteering on a project abroad might be. And a *Go and Help* grant — freephone 0800-842842:

The Prince's Trust, 18 Park Square East, London NW1 4LH, UK

CCIVS/*Coordinating Committee for International Voluntary Service,* c/o UNESCO, 1 rue Miollis, 75732, Paris cédex 15, *France* — *UK* tel 01206-298215 — coordinates international volunteer projects and also workcamps with partner organizations around the world. See section 2.32 in *Getting a Job,* and under '*IVS*' *(or 'SVI / SCI')* in your own local phone book. Also *Direct Contacts ...*

Also see 'Voluntary work,' Personal Experiences

Work experience. Contact the *British Council* and the *Central Bureau* — tel 0207-389 4004 — see the address under *Year off* over the page — about work, exchange and volunteer schemes; also in the *Getting a job* chapter — and you can call — or go and visit — a British Council office in some very far-flung locations.

If you are from *Portugal,* write to the 'links officer for Portugal' at the Central Bureau — from anywhere in the world — if you are from *Spain* '. . . for Spain,' and so on. These organizations in *Britain* share the same address: 10 Spring Gardens, London SW1A 2BN, UK; also enclosing a self-addressed envelope.

Their *Youth Exchange Centre* number is 0207-385 4030; otherwise tel 0207-389 4004; fax 0207-389 4426.

And internationally, *AIESEC*, 40 rue Washington, 1050 Brussels, *Belgium*; tel +32-(0)2-6462420 (UK tel 0207-336 7939) is *"an independent, non profit-making and non-political organization run entirely by students"* — the *Association Internationale des Étudiants en Sciences Économiques et Commerciales* — with an international exchange scheme for six or eight-week periods, in 80 different countries. *For further information on this, ask at your college or university*

X . . .

Year off. This might be a year away from your normal job, or before university. Otherwise known as a 'gap year' — see 2.32 — maybe what Leonardo DiCaprio is doing in 'The Beach' . . .

Some useful leaflets are produced by the *Central Bureau for Educational Visits and Exchanges* — see above — 10 Spring Gardens, London SW1A 2BN, UK

Zookeeping. No news about that. I did see an interesting programme on TV about a vet working in a wildlife sanctuary in *Zimbabwe* once though.

These are some of the literally hundreds of ideas you can follow

up and jobs you can do. The person it depends on is you

International workers 1.7

There are two main types of migration in the world. But these two groups of international migrants will not always be the same people, doing the same kinds of job. Far from it — and there is a much more important fact which will face you if you areworkingabroad, whereveryoucomefrom.Quitesimply, it depends on your skills and qualifications — so if you are a doctor, you can be a doctor almost anywhere — and part-time, casual, badly paid work is not unknown in the richer countries of the world either.

Some will be concerned about visas — and the different ways you can enter a country to work are discussed later (under *Work permits and residence permits* and *Visas* — 1.22 and 1.24). In theory, this is quite straightforward — this system for visas is also an 'international' one. And the laws of each country for visas, emigration and tax are also linked, much more so than people realize — part of a global system.

The principles, if not the rules, for working abroad are the same almost everywhere. But in each country, even within the European Union *for instance, the details will be different*

The EU 1.8

In the European Union — and *Iceland*, *Liechtenstein* and *Norway* which are not actually members of the EU but part of the wider *European Economic Area* — if you are from one of these countries — and you can speak the language, which will help — you can live, work, and study — and even be unemployed — in any other EEA / EU country: *Austria, Belgium, Czech Republic (joining), Denmark, Estonia (joining), France, Finland, Germany, Greece, Hungary (joining), Ireland, Italy, Luxembourg, The Netherlands, Poland (joining), Portugal, Slovenia (joining), Spain, Sweden, and the UK, in the* European Union — *as well as Iceland, Liechtenstein and Norway in the* EEA

The world 1.9

Geographically speaking, we all know what it looks like: the twin continents of North and South America, Europe, Africa and Asia, Australasia, and then Oceania, and the region of the Arctic and the continent which is *Antarctica*. Unless you are off to the South Pole — and come to think of it there are cruises to the Arctic or Antarctic nowadays — then we can rule out these last two, leaving the world's more temperate and tropical places. This is where we will go to live and work.

And leaving aside the possibility that you might end up as an entertainer on a cruise liner going to the Antarctic — in one of the most remote regions of the earth . . . from the point of view of working in general we can consider the more likely scenario of a map of the world according to wealth: the Gross Domestic Product of each country; and how much each one earns.

This gives another picture of the world we live — and work — in

The world according to wealth 1.10

What would happen if we considered each country according to the size of its economic wealth? On such a map, the Polar regions have gone — but you might be shocked to find that so too —

almost — has Africa — with 1.4% of the world's GDP — now just a tiny economic addition to Europe. And Oceania means just two small countries: *Australia* and *New Zealand* (1.5%) — which have about the same GDP as the whole of Africa. On a global scale, the rest of this Pacific / Oceania region is virtually invisible.

And we can see how tiny *Canada* is (2%) — compared to its geographical size, but still a medium-sized economic power — and how Latin America is just a small area (4%) — mainly *Brazil* — attached physically but we can see also economically to the *United States*.

Europe has some fair-sized countries. *Britain* is larger than you might expect (4% — equivalent in this percentage of world GDP to the whole of Latin America); *France* is large (5%); and largest of all is *Germany* (8%) — *Russia* again seems tiny by comparison (1.5%). Central and Eastern Europe (1.5%), and the Middle East (1.2%) — these seem to be economically dependent areas too.

In Asia, Central Asia is another very small region; and even countries like *India* and *China* (1.2% and 3%) are much smaller than *Japan*, with 16% of the world's total Gross Domestic Product.

Not everybody in the rich countries is rich, or in poor countries is poor. But there are these two main economic zones in the world, the 'rich-zone' countries and the 'poor-zone' countries

The developing world 1.11

And those in the middle, too, which used to be called the developing countries. They still have populations which are often very poor. These 'middling' countries might include places like *North Africa* and *Brazil.* Then there are places of absolute poverty like sub-Saharan Africa (excluding the Maghreb / Northern Africa and the *Republic of South Africa).*

This has sometimes been known as the Fourth World — excluded from the world economy. Of those which have been classified as the heavily indebted poor countries (these have an acronym — HIPCs) all, apart from *Bolivia, Guyana, Honduras, Laos, Myanmar, Nicaragua, Vietnam* and *Yemen*, are in Africa.

This has a direct impact on the question of living and working abroad. In *Japan*, the country earns on average $34,000 per annum per person; and owes nothing. In the *USA*, these figures are $30,000, and $3,500, considering the national wealth. In a place like *Angola* or *Zambia*, this annual turnover — not any idea of the 'profit' the country makes, but the turnover — is much less than its total debt.

Which is also where the greatest unemployment is

The world according to unemployment 1.12

This is mainly in Africa, the sub-Saharan countries (12% of the world's total), and also in Iran (3%), India (1%) and in Asia and Latin America, with a high percentage also in Eastern Europe.

This imbalance of wealth and employment is growing, in poorer countries and rich ones alike

The three 'pillars' of the world economy 1.13

Somehow there are three main trading zones, within this larger world economy. And wealth is concentrated in three main geographical areas: North America, Europe, and East Asia. There is a pattern — really a patchwork — of wealth and poverty in these three main areas. Which are:

the Americas; Europe / Africa ; Middle East / and Asia; Oceania

These are the three main geographical 'pillars', as they are sometimes described, supporting the world economy

Six degrees of immigration 1.14

And all these issues apply locally as well as globally. This imbalance between wealth and employment can be a local issue — on the level of countries, towns, villages, the drift of populations to the town from the countryside . . . but this is also a worldwide concern. It is mirrored in relations between the *United States* and the countries of Latin America, say, or *Japan* and *China*.

So it will depend on where you come from, and where you are going, as to what kind of trip this will this be, to live and work in another country. You might be moving from the *Philippines* to Japan — where there is still a need for labour (even if there is more unemployment there than there used to be). Or from one of the countries of Central America to the United States for similar reasons, to get on in life and better yourself.

The same might apply to someone from North Africa living in *France;* and in reverse for all these three main economic areas of the world, from South to North as well as North to South. But this time it is because qualifications, skills, and education are needed

— in terms of economic development, and not just for self-advancement.

If you went from *France* to *Libya* to be an oil engineer for example, it might be like this; or from one of the countries of Western Europe to Central Asia. Activities in these 'developing' countries are often in these 'primary' areas of agriculture or the extractive industries.

Someone from the *USA* might be a mining engineer in Latin America — and be able to do this because of a skills shortage locally. *Korean* companies could invest in *Kazakstan* and send staff there for similar reasons — as indeed they have.

This is part of a general pattern. Living and working abroad reflects these larger issues of global development or scant resources, and the investment in / exploitation of the poorer countries by the rich ones. Questions you will also come across if you are living and working abroad

Opportunities and restrictions 1.15

There will be opportunities but also restrictions in this new place. Some will move for more altruistic reasons; but many will go for their own benefit, to live somewhere where the cost of living is less, or they can get on in life, or property is more affordable — or to have a life which is more one of leisure and less of work.

Britons used to think of the Mediterranean like this, as a good place to retire to, or have a more leisurely lifestyle in. This could be classed as an 'opportunity' in this economic sense.

One main difference when you are crossing borders for work is in your earning power — which can go up or down according to the circumstances. In many areas of technical, scientific or other expertise, international workers will find that this goes up when they are abroad.

Others are the barriers which still exist for immigration or trade, even within the larger trading zones like the EU (1.8) or ASEAN (the Association of South-East Asian Nations). An opportunity for some, and a restriction for others.

Qualifications and skills are the main reason you can cross these barriers — or a skills gap, where you have an ability which is not readily available in that place — being a translator or a language teacher say

Others will accept less highly paid jobs. Or move because they have a business, or want to start one — or they can even invest in the country, to have a steady source of income in retirement

The job and your career 1.16

You might accept less pay to do a challenging new job — one you wouldn't even think you might have the opportunity to do in your own country — or expect to be paid more to make up for the difficulties of moving there.

You could be going for your more long-term career, and be ready to make some financial sacrifices; or accept the limitations of where you are now compared to where you want to be and have a very poorly paid job.

Wherever you go, you should think carefully about going just for the privilege of being able to stay in another country. The job — and your career — is important too

Finding out more 1.17

Here are some places where you could find out more about what you need to know about your chosen career or country — a better approach in this age of rapid changes in both work and travel than just writing off to any old list of addresses.

Some good places to contact first of all are:

Embassies and Consulates

National Tourist Offices

Chambers of Commerce

You can also find out about working there from professional associations and trade unions

Embassies and Consulates 1.18

These are the representatives of that country in your country. Or, when you get there, your country there. Which is obvious enough. But what does an embassy do?

One role is to help its own citizens abroad, when they are travelling — or living, or doing business. So they might have quite a close connection with the community of its citizens there — and be a good source of information about joint chambers of commerce for instance, or trade associations — also for rules for importing and exporting; also for the rules for people who have moved there.

What is the difference between an embassy and a consulate? Embassies are the main diplomatic delegation, with their office — which will usually be sovereign territory — in the capital city: in the *USA* in Washington; in *Russia* in Moscow . . . Consulates are mainly in other towns and places; to be contacted if you are going to that particular city or town.

Embassies look after the interests of their country in that country. Consulates look after the interests of its people there. So, of course, there is a consulate in the capital too. This might be called the 'consular section' of the embassy.

Consulates tend to deal with visas and passports, even work regulations; and would probably have some useful information to give you about this. This might be called the 'consular' or 'visa department' at the main embassy.

Or there may be a separate consulate where you are, of that country in your country — which deals with visa applications, and not the embassy itself. In either case, you should contact the consulate of the place you are going to — where you are now — and also your own consulate there, on the spot.

The embassy can always put you through, or give you their number.

In general, your enquiry should be addressed to the 'visa section' — which should get it to the right place — or the 'commercial counsellor' — or the 'labour counsellor' — or even 'to whom it may concern.' If you visit there or telephone, do so in the morning, as many visa sections shut early in the afternoons

Contacting the embassy 1.19

Even the way they respond to your inquiry can tell you some-thing about the country. The Embassy of the Republic of *Armenia* in London, for example, offers the following excellent photocopied notes — 'Guidance for Persons Intending to Travel to Armenia' — informing you that:

"The capital of Armenia is Yerevan (old name Erebouni, Russian name Erivan), which has a population of about 1.5 million and a metro system . . . Other large towns are Kumairi (ex Leninakhan) and Vanadzor (ex Kirovakan) . . .

The centre of the Armenian Church is the Cathedral of Echmiadzin, about 20 km west of Yerevan . . . Travellers intending to visit Armenia should bear in mind that on entering the country they become subject to the jurisdiction of a State with a social, political and judicial system different from that of their own. Some activities which may be legal in your own country may be regarded as offences in Armenia."

Which is one warning to all working travellers, wherever they go. You will be living in the country and subject to the local laws. This kind of information, which embassies can send you — especially for countries where there have been recent changes in names, official language and the political system — will be the most reliable and up to date, much more so than any guide book. This is what you need.

There then follow sections on 'Visas', 'Visiting Relatives', 'Travel into Armenia', 'Air Travel', 'Accommodation and Food', 'Currency and Customs Regulations', 'Health', 'Climate', 'Electrical Supply', 'Water', 'Language', 'History and Historic Monuments' — all of which you need to know — and reads like a basic checklist of what you should find out about when you are travelling to a new or 'unknown' location, somewhere you have never been before.

Which might be your situation when you are off to live and work in another country. You always need the most up-to-date sources of information

Working there 1.20

Where else can you go to find out about working there? That country's embassy may not see it as their job to help people from other countries get a job, or help you to emigrate — and may actively be seeking to discourage this. This might well be so for some of the more prosperous countries of the world; but all have their rules and regulations to follow and sensitivities to observe.

Workers sent to the 'developing' countries by aid organizations should be just as skilled and qualified. And many poorer countries may not appreciate aid and development — and an influx of workers — which is misdirected and misconceived. Nor would they automatically grant international workers a work permit either. Why should they?

But many still need workers in areas where skills are needed or where there is a labour shortage

Your embassy on the spot 1.21

Also contact your embassy on the spot. For example, the British Consul in Ljubljana, *Slovenia*, can supply "*both British and Commonwealth citizens*" with a useful 'Registration Pack' which is intended for new residents there but useful for anyone as part of their preparation. Services provided by the Consulate include the issuing of passports, registration of births and deaths and 'notarial acts' (e.g. authorizing or stamping documents for official use, and liaising in all these important matters with national and local government organizations back home).

The contents of this useful *Registration Pack for Slovenia* are a good example of the kind of information your consulate or embassy should be able to provide when you are going to another country to live and work:

Residence permits

Work and business visas

Housing agencies and hotels

English-speaking doctors, dentists, lawyers

Payment of income tax

Church services

Ex-Pats Anonymous (a local club)

Electoral Registration Forms (to keep up your right to vote at home)

A *Slovene-British Society leaflet (an independent association)*

Useful information and points of interest

A *map*

Car Rental services

and *International Money Transfer services*

Your embassy or consulate on the spot should be able to tell you a lot about living and working there. So can chambers of commerce and national tourist offices

Work permits and residence permits 1.22

'Do I need a work permit as well as a residence permit?' is one question you can ask when making your enquiry for where to go to get a work permit or residence visa — which you should do — and asking how to do this.

For many — for EU citizens travelling and working within the European Union countries for instance — all the way from *Portugal* to *Poland* — soon — with *Estonia*, the *Czech Republic*, *Hungary* and *Slovenia* — a work permit will not be needed in any of these places. But this is not quite the end of the matter — as you will still have to register as a resident, and have somewhere to live — an address there; and not be just on holiday.

International workers — and the local people themselves — will also need to carry some kind of identity card

On arrival 1.23

In the EU it is easy. You just need to go — and register with the local town hall or police station. You just need a residence permit — not a work permit — meaning you will just need somewhere to live. If you can speak the language — and are suitably qualified and experienced — which will help — you can live, work and study — and even be unemployed — in any other EU / EEA country — if you are an EU citizen of course.

This is for citizens and people from EU / EEA *countries. For others it will be more difficult*

Visas 1.24

Tourist visas and business visas. Visas are really a permit, a permission to enter the country between certain dates. When countries don't ask for visas this means you can go there for as long as you like — but not necessarily to work. This is where work and residence permits come in.

Confused? It really is quite straightforward. If you have a business visa, you can do business in that country — an area which can seem like work, but work is when you are paid a salary, not just a fee for goods or services. If you have a tourist visa, you can go there for tourism, but you are not doing business or working.

But there is no rule which says this holiday means you have to stay on the beach, and do nothing . . . And you can research your options and find out more, and research the possibility of getting a job

Education visas. If you can find out about the education system or universities you can apply to — in a country like *France*, where the fees for foreign students are still relatively cheap — and if you gain acceptance on a course, then you should be able to get a visa for this, or for any similar education course.

Your work becomes a part-time way of supporting yourself while you are there.

Difficult, but thousands of students from Africa and Latin America know about this way of living and working abroad, from the *USA* to the *Former Soviet Union*.

Often a first visit to another country will be as a tourist — this applies across the spectrum of living and working abroad, from the proud owner of a new property in the South of France to a student from Nigeria *studying at the local university. Many will have been there on vacation before*

Passports 1.25

The main point is, there are some countries where you can go where you don't need a visa, just a passport — and even with just your national identity card if you have European Union citizenship or residency it is possible to get from one EU country to another — but take your passport just in case.

And when you get a visa, certainly make the dates of your stay generous enough to include all eventualities. Leaving a country with a visa which has run out is tricky. They will check it on departure — in effect you will probably have to buy another one

Regulations for work permits – USA 1.26

A 'post-it' note from the *United States Information Agency* at the *US Embassy* on the document in front of me says: "*Here is what is available, however, to obtain specific information you will have to access the Embassy website at a library.*"

"*Welcome to the American Embassy's Visa Services Homepage, providing information on visa requirements for travelers to the* United States *who wish to visit, work, or study for a temporary period, and those who wish to take up indefinite residence*" — from a printout which they kindly sent.

"*Written information is available from the* Visa Branch, *5 Upper Grosvenor Street, London, W1A 2JB,* UK. *A stamped addressed envelope must accompany the request. We regret we are unable to respond to inquiries received by e-mail.*" As you would be unwise to call; their 'operator assisted visa information service' costs £1.50 per minute.

You can choose, then, from 'Immigrant Visas' or 'Non Immigrant Visas' . . .

"*The following is a list of the main topics covered by our web page,*" they say:

— *Applying for a nonimmigrant visa*

— *List of Travel agents*

- — *The B-1 visa for business*
- — *The B-2 visa for tourism*
- — *Visa requirements for academics, researchers and exchange students*
- — *Student (F-1 and M-1) visas*
- — *Exchange visitor (J-1) visas*
- — *Employment Based Visas*
- — *Visa requirements for members of the media*
- — *Visa requirements for members of the entertainment professions, athletes and persons with extraordinary ability in the sciences, arts, education and business*
- — *Visa requirements for Ministers of religion and religious workers*
- — *Visa requirements for au pairs, nannies, and mother's helpers*"

The US embassy website (in the UK) is:
www.usembassy.org.uk/

For people wishing to live or work more permanently in the *United States* there are three ways of doing it: either for family-sponsored, employment-based, or 'diversity' immigration (more commonly known as the Green Card lottery). You have to be closely related to a US citizen to qualify as a relative, not a grandparent, grandchild, aunt, uncle, cousin or in-law.

Employment-based immigration can cover 'priority workers' — those of "*extraordinary ability*" mentioned above, like university professors, managers, outstanding athletes . . . Or members of the professions, and "*professionals and skilled and unskilled workers*"

— but these must have relevant qualifications or skills which are in short supply in the *United States* — and so in fact only highly skilled workers will get there this way.

And finally, 'investors': "*those creating employment for at least ten persons and investing a minimum of $1,000,000 in a new commercial enterprise.*"

"*And an annual* 'Diversity Immigration Program' *makes available each year by random selection 55,000 immigrant visas to people from countries with low rates of immigration to the* United States. *Eligibility to apply for this program is determined by a person's place of birth, not citizenship.*"

The registration period for this 'Green Card' lottery is usually in October; and certain exclusions will apply.

Non-immigrant visas for employment. These work visas would be usually obtained with the help of the employer in the United States and need the approval of the Immigration and Naturalization Service (INS) on the basis of a petition. This is if you are going there for a shorter time or not going there permanently. You would receive a 1—797 A or B form, then, to present to the Embassy when making your application for this work permit.

What kind of visa? 1.27

For everybody, nearly everywhere, it boils down to something like this: if I go there with a tourist or visitor's visa, or with an education visa, or a business visa, can I get work? Or do I have to get a work visa before I go?

The answer is, if you are going there to take up a job which has been arranged for you, you will need to get this sorted out before you go — or the person arranging this for you at your company should. It should be quite straightforward if the organization already has an operation or branch there, and there is someone to make the application for you; and then send you the form — the 'notice of action' form it is called in the *United States* — which you can take to the embassy to show your application has been approved. Of course, this may take time . . .

Otherwise, to get a job there, you can make your application on arrival. You can do this almost anywhere — and the very worst that can happen is that you would then have to make a trip to the nearest third country to sort out all these procedures properly; and come back again after another visit to your embassy there — if some kind of document needs to be stamped for instance — for an education course you have signed up for, say. Or if you are travelling on business — or travelling around a lot — maybe getting a 'multi-entry visa' is a good idea.

You might also need a 'sponsor', to support your application, — an individual, or maybe a company, or family member there. A co-operative local employer can be helpful. More usually, when you get a job almost anywhere, it will just mean you join the queue at the local work office / employment service, or *Ministry of the Interior / Home Office,* to let them know.

When you go abroad to find or take up work on a speculative basis, you should always take enough money to allow for unexpected expenses — like a trip abroad to renew your visa

A list of contacts 1.28

And while you are making your preparations, keep a list of personal contacts for that country, beginning with the person or people you speak to at the embassy — in your own country and also when you get there.

You may not know these people well; but even knowing their names — like that of the local ambassador — can help if you do find yourself in a tricky situation abroad

National Tourist Offices 1.29

This may not be the first place you think of if you are looking for a job in another country. It should be. And if you can get past the premium-rate phone line you can find out much more about anything from the driving conditions to the system of government. Your source is simply your local *Yellow Pages;* where you can look under 'tourist offices;' or look in the phone book under the name of the country, e.g. 'Spanish Tourist Office.' (And see *Getting there* under *Driving*, where there is more about *Switzerland* and *Germany* and their respective tourist offices).

Many of these, unfortunately, do have their more expensive premium-rate numbers, making their service more 'efficient' — and making money — and used for automatically sending out brochures or dealing with standard inquiries. But yours is not; so try to get through on the regular line with your more specific enquiry.

This will save money, and help you beat the queue — another trick of successful travel

Local tourist information offices 1.30

Most local places where you will be will also have a local tourist information office — the national tourist office could tell you where quite easily. But if not, try the main tourist organization — the one in that country — which is another way to get through to a more local one. Write and ask for brochures and information relating to your trip there. You can find out where various tourism associations and organizations are from the embassy also.

Also request any 'What's On' magazines, local publications, and local maps they may have — some more useful acquisitions while you are still planning your trip

A preliminary visit 1.31

Visiting the country, town, or place, is really a good idea. You can do a number of things depending on your circumstances:

Look for a job

Visit your workplace

Visit any friends or family there

Make financial arrangements

Prepare for your move

You can also find out more about accommodation / education / immigration / work / tax, or anything else like this, perhaps by visiting your embassy there. And see more about this in Chapter 2 on *Getting a job*.

While you are there, you may have your own contacts for work or your business, or family and friends you can look up. Or be travelling with your family

Travelling with your family 1.32

If you can spend some time in that place before your move, this will be one of the best ways to prepare for the adventure which lies ahead. One intrepid traveller recently took his family on a trip around the world by horse-drawn caravan . . . so it can be done — and wrote a book about it: *The Seven-Year Hitch — A Family Odyssey*, by David R. Grant (Simon and Schuster).

A good book about how to travel with your children is Travel Without Tears, *published by Need2Know guides, by Marion Jayawardene; available in most libraries; or bookshops; and also through similar internet bookstores.*

They also publish The Expatriate Experience — a practical guide to successful relocation, *by Bobby Meyer.*

Many other travel books and books about living and working abroad are listed in Appendix 2, Sources of Information

Salaries 1.33

Working — anywhere — at the bottom end of the salary scale is hard — which is what working visitors often tend to underestimate.

But for many the motive is economic — to get a job in another country and earn enough to live, and save too. And not everyone working abroad is interested in just an interesting lifestyle and travel.

Lowering your wage expectations if you live in a different country — too much — is not such a good idea. But international workers will very often have to do this

Legislation 1.34

There will also be legislation covering your employment rights, health and safety, a minimum wage, discrimination, hours of work, holidays, and so on; and many other rights which would apply to international workers — and you — and not just to local people. But if you have a legal problem at work, you are going to need the advice of a lawyer, or trade union, who can help.

The Ministry of Labour *or* Employment *— or local employment services — would be a contact for the labour laws. Or national trade union association, there may be one — or many, with different political affiliations*

Tax 1.35

You will need a tax number. And to keep a record of your pay, payslips, the name and address of your employer, and the tax office ... Unless you will be there just for a few weeks, or doing a casual job, most people who going abroad to live and work should think about this too. Also see Chapter 5, 5.12 .

The standard arrangement for tax — if you live abroad for up to 182 days in any one year — or perhaps an average of 90 days per year over five years — is that you do not become a resident for these purposes, if you are there for this short time, usually anything up to six months or a year. But you are still liable to pay tax on your income there.

And then you may be liable to pay once again — a second time — in your own country. So find out if there is a 'double taxation agreement' between the two countries. This will stop your income being taxed twice

Tax avoidance 1.36

Importing and exporting have their own tax rules too — involving paying customs duty — and the same general points I have mentioned above about tax and payment apply to businesses too, depending on where the person or business is based. This would either be in one country or the other; if you are involved in trade for instance. If you have a house there, that may already make you a resident of that country as far as the tax authorities are concerned.

But no-one can be a resident of both places; and everyone is a resident of somewhere. This is the basic principle — and the reason for the 182-day rule. If you are going there for 183 days, that makes more than half a year . . . And the question of when you leave is also an important one — or when you start your business — or buy your house — which may be half way through your own country's tax year; perhaps nearer the end of that of the country you are moving to.

In this overlapping period, you might be able to take advantage of the full tax allowances of both countries. So, is the tax year from April to March — or January to December — where you are going? When should you arrive? And if you buy property, would you be classed as a resident from that date?

The point is that the reach of the tax man — or person — is as long as that of the law. Tax planning is a good idea; but tax avoidance is not. Only in very rare cases — for diplomats and armed services personnel, for instance — perhaps for the fishing industry, where this takes place in foreign waters — can you be somewhere abroad, and *not* be liable to pay tax: for income, for capital gains, for companies, for property, for social security, for any kind of money you have coming in.

As a general rule, any employer who does not pay tax — or register that you are working for them — has an unreasonable power over you. And it is probable you will only be there for part of your first tax year — and that you do not earn too much anyway . . . If you work for a short time — or earn under the tax threshold there, or are in the lowest tax band — it may be that you will not have to pay much in any case.

So it is better, in all ways, to register your presence in the country. For more about residency, see the Living abroad *chapter*

Keeping a record of things like your pay slips, and bank statements, and tax and social security numbers, is also very important, from the day you arrive in a new country

And one of the first things you should do if you are emigrating for longer than a year — or even over six months of that particular tax year — is to inform your own tax / social security / national insurance office of the change — and not try to avoid this. They will advise you

Information services 1.37

You can find out more about tax for individuals and companies by contacting the consulate — or the labour or visa department at the embassy — or, best of all, their trade or commercial office.

Or *English Contacts Abroad* (PO Box 126, Oxford OX2 6AU, UK) which provides a full service of information about visas, trade, travel, immigration and work in more than 100 countries — as well as for English teaching work. You would be sent a questionnaire where you can include all the details you think are relevant — and just a short letter of inquiry is OK in the first instance — the fee being £48.

Or send a copy of the English Contacts Abroad *questionnaire in this book —* *p.114* *— along with your inquiry*

Different people, different cultures, different expectations 1.38

Working in another country, you may find you are meeting more different kinds of people — as well as having a changed set of expectations in the area of work — and what you earn. Abroad, it is true that you can earn much less — or much more — than at home; and your position may be more precarious, riskier. But you cannot expect your life to remain exactly as it was before.

You will have to change your own expectations. And the kind of expectations other people have of you will certainly change too, when you are living and working abroad

Sources of information about employment abroad 1.39

An interesting report each year on the world economy and trends in each country is published in French – ramses 2000 – synthèse annuelle de l'évolution du monde, *published by* Dunod *and the* institut français des relations internationales (ifri), *27 rue de la Procession, 75740 Paris Cedex, France. Here you will find an overview of politics, economics, and issues seen on a global scale; and maps of the world based on population growth, urbanization, riches and poverty, conflicts, and risks; RAMSES being the* Rapport Annuel Mondial sur le Système Economique et les Stratégies

There are also some Personal Experiences *in Appendix 3 of people who have worked or stayed in another country for a short, medium, or long time*

Overseas Jobs Express *newspaper — and its website — will give you a good idea of the range of job opportunities worldwide, in everything from accountancy to au pair work — but not quite to zookeeping — and also tell you what it is like to go and live and work abroad.*

OJE, *tel 01273-440220/540, fax 01273-440229, e-mail editor@overseasjobs.com, http:* **www.overseasjobs.com**

Subscribers also receive their publication Work Abroad

The International Association of Antarctic Tour Operators (IAATO), *Suite 110, 111 East 14th Street, New York, NY 10003; tel 212-460-8715; fax 212-529-8684; e-mail iaato@iaato.org;* www.iaato.org *— for that Antarctic cruise job*

See Appendix 2 for some Sources of Information *about work abroad; and Appendix 1* Direct Contacts *for some more useful contacts*

In 'The Beach' *by Alex Garland (Penguin), Richard finds himself alone and abroad almost by accident — a salutary tale — but you can learn from experience, during all these stages*

Key Points

And take some time out now to think about where you are starting from — and what are your aims or intentions:

1. Think of your career

2. Think about jobs you can do

3. Make the plans for your trip

4. Consider what will happen when you arrive

5. Find out more about the country

2

Getting a job

"Think not just what you can do for your job — but what your job can do for you"

Leonardo DiCaprio in 'The Beach' didn't do much. Work, that is — or preparation. But you are going to have to. This chapter is on getting a job abroad — with many suggestions for how to do this, beginning with some 'Sources of Jobs.'

Also see the List of Contents — *and the* Introduction — *for more on how to use this book and the subjects covered in each chapter*

Sources of jobs 2.1

In fact, most job vacancies are filled not by someone painstakingly sifting through large numbers of applicants; or a personnel department carefully checking through all your references. Or even by the kind of companies you can find lists of; and then sending out hundreds of application letters (which will either be filed away or thrown away).

Contacting someone they know directly is simpler and more reliable from the employer's point of view. Who needs someone to do the job — then contacts someone about it. This is how it is for getting a job — and is the major source of most jobs anywhere. So you have to make yourself known to the right people. To be the person *they* know; and try to get to know them too.

This is what recruitment departments of large companies are trying to do too, in a way, when they visit colleges and universities, 'getting to know people' — which is what they do: creating a pool of potential labour from which vacancies can then be filled.

You can try to get to know them too, and use some of the methods they use

Making an application 2.2

First of all, you need to get to know about the vacancy — and the company / agency / organization — and then narrow it down, this potentially huge number of options and employers you have.

You don't have to contact them too hastily if a job is advertised — there are sharks out there . . . without thinking if this is something you really want to do. So give yourself time.

And the job should come first if you are looking for a job abroad, not just the destination, even an island in the sun . . .

Taking your chances 2.3

And present yourself to your best advantage; and prepare a CV (UK English) or résumé (US English) and general letter of application in advance, so you are ready to apply — and also send off some inquiry / enquiry letters.

What kind of CV do you need? Again it depends on what you want to do. Some employers and agencies will probably look at your résumé in a rather literal-minded way — seeing it as a list of qualifications, skills, experience . . . starting with your most recent.

Others will pick out one element which appeals; and then this will be an opportunity — if you see things this way — for you to tell them in more depth about your interests, skills, and what you want to do. It depends on how you look at it too, on knowing yourself and who you are (4.3).

A translation into the other language might be a good idea — but is not strictly speaking necessary if the job involves using your own.

Again you will have to choose the best opportunities for you, and not just accept any which might come your way

A letter of inquiry 2.4

You can send off a letter of inquiry, first of all — or by fax or e-mail — and maybe ask for an application form. You could also telephone — 'Do they want a CV or maybe there is a form to fill in?' might be one question to ask — and also find out more about the vacancy or the organization.

This kind of direct approach is often a good one. And all kinds of business like this are best carried out in the mornings, and nearer the beginning of the week — which would probably be the most effective time for you to contact them

Sending CVs 2.5

If you are sending a letter — or fax — or e-mail — you can enclose — or attach — your CV — the aim of which is to tell them you are a good candidate, someone worth meeting. And this is not just a formula to follow — many jobs are obtained without one. Sometimes a letter will be enough: one offering to visit — or telling them more about yourself and the skills you can offer, and when you will be there — and using a phrase like "*I would like to highlight the following skills which I can offer to your organization*" — and not a full CV.

Say when you will be visiting, or available to meet

A visit there 2.6

This would be a good way — as you would need to go in any case if you are thinking about living and working in a particular country. So, if you want a job abroad, you could carry out your job search there, on the spot.

Try to get an interview before you go. And very rarely will just a CV you sent off get you the job by itself — would this be one you wanted anyway?

You would need to send a letter — or fax, or e-mail — and then arrange interviews / meetings with potential employers — who will be interested in your motivation and reasons for doing the job, as well as your presence in the country. Or should be. Just living abroad, and your wish to enjoy a different climate or way of life will not usually be enough from their point of view.

On your preliminary visit, you could arrange other aspects of your stay like accommodation, and find out more about the place

Before your interview 2.7

Before any interview, some other tips are to:

Cultivate contacts — as this interview, even if you do not get this job, could be a source of others in the future

And ask questions — about the salary, or when a decision might be made

At the end, thank the person who interviewed you

When you arrive, greet reception staff politely — not just the interviewer!

Also, keep your replies simple. Don't try too hard to impress

Dress neatly, and in a way you feel comfortable with

Seven ways of getting a job abroad 2.8

Here are seven ways of getting a job, anywhere you go.

1. Employment services (2.9). Through the local state or national employment service — which in Britain is the Jobcentre. This is where unemployed people register or sign on (for those not acquainted with them).

But they also have a service as a source of local employment — not always specialist jobs like translation, or the law — where you can imagine employers might contact someone else — but the more general local ones, in catering, or security, or whatever — mine-clearance jobs in *Kuwait* is one which sticks in the memory — and maybe there are some more user-friendly ones like working in local restaurants, bars, shops; and also seasonal work, before Christmas or in the tourist season . . . for that job as a shopping mall Santa or ski rep . . . In the EU (European Union), this system is not supposed to help visitors from outside the *EU / EEA* countries — in theory. But an on-the-spot job search and visit would be useful, wherever you go and wherever you are from. And this is one way to find out about the general and also some specialist work which is going.

In the *USA*, there are national and state employment services (see 2.11 below).

Where to find out about the employment service there? Use a little ingenuity, perhaps by contacting the embassy or their cultural information centre. Or visit your own local *Jobcentre / employment service*, which should help.

The local Yellow Pages will be easy to find if you are on a visit. Try a local post office, which may have phone books for inspection (but not now in *Britain*). Or at your hotel. Visiting the employment service — and companies / organizations / recruitment agencies — is also a good idea.

And if you don't speak the language, you might need a friend who can come along — although there are a lot of careers advisers in places like *Sweden* and *Spain* who now speak English or other languages — and language ability is important for you too — see 4.14. But it is quite surprising, sometimes, how much of a job advertisement in another country you can understand, even in a language you don't know well.

You can go along; or ask for the address for the employment service there beforehand — for example the Ministry of Employment *would have it. Or send them a fax and they will usually be able to send you addresses of local offices or* bureaux

International vacancy notification 2.10

In the *EU / EEA* countries, there is also a quicker way. Each one, now, also has a nationwide system of vacancy notification — which can tell you about jobs in all the European Union countries, wherever you are. So, your local *Jobcentre* in the *UK* really can tell you about jobs from *Ireland* to *Estonia*. And vice versa.

In *Britain*, *Employment Service Direct* is their national 'helpline' number — which can do a search by country or profession as well as in your local area, a service for unemployed people to "*get you a full or part-time job.*"

Employment Service Direct: telephone 0845-6060-234; website *www.employmentservice.gov.uk*

With or without a national insurance / social security number they can do a job search for you — and for some more high-level professional and trade jobs which tend to be notified to them by foreign employment *bureaux* — as well as more general ones.

The links between employment services are one practical benefit of the EU's aim of making jobs all across Europe available to European Union citizens — and one which might help some visitors from outside the EU too

Getting through to the employment service 2.11

In *America*, it is the *US Department of Labor — Employment and Training Administration* (*www.doleta.gov*) or the *Public Employment Service* (*www.ajb.dni.us*). In *Australia*, *Australian Job Search*, and also the government employment service, can be contacted through *www.jobsearch.gov.au*.

Or at least someone in this chain of inquiry I have mentioned can send you a list of local offices of the employment service where you are going. The Internet is a very powerful way of finding out about this kind of organization; but not the only one. Their embassies, or the *Ministry of Employment*, must certainly have the main employment service address. And any other information you might get about the country along the way can be useful too.

Or just find the right name to look up in the local phone book or *Yellow Pages* (to be found in embassies, libraries . . .).

On the internet, the contact for the network of employment services in the EU is:

http:*//www.europa.eu.int/jobs/eures*

In *Austria*, your local Jobcentre is a *Landesarbeitsamt;* and the employment service is the *Arbeitsmarktservice Österreich (AMS)*

In *Belgium* the *T-service* is where you go — part of the *FOREM* (French-speaking employment service) or the *VDAB* (Flemish-speaking version). And the *Office Régional Bruxellois de l'Emploi* is a different employment service in the capital, known as ORBEM (on the internet at *www.orbem.be*)

In *Denmark*, *Arbejdsformidlingen* are the 'jobcentres' — *www.af.dk*

The French national employment service is the *Agence Nationale pour l'Emploi (ANPE)* — 4 rue Galilée, 93198 Noisy-le-Grand, *France; tel +1-49 31 77 11*. They can send you a list of their *agences locales*. Also at *www.anpe.fr*.

The *Centre d'Information et de Documentation Jeunesse* —

CIDJ — 101 quai Branly, 75740 Paris, can tell you more about work for young people

In *Finland*, it is a *työvoimatoimisto*, run by the *Työhallinon Palvelut (ML)* — *www.mol.fi*

In *Germany*, *Arbeitsamter*

In *Greece*, the *OAED — European Section* can give you access to their employment services: tel +30-1-9942-2466 (direct); or the switchboard number we have is +30-1-9989500, fax +30-1-9989500; Ethinikis Antistasis 8, 166 10A Glyfada, Greece — *www.eie.org.gr* for the National Labour Institute

In the *Netherlands*, *Arbeidsbureau* . . .

Also, you could do your own research in your own local Jobcentre or elsewhere about where these employment services (not to be confused with private sector job agencies which may have similar names) are to be found.

This is simply to illustrate the general principle here — and to show how the system works — not just locally in your country, but increasingly internationally; so that each employment service in each country can also give you contacts for another one. Even your local one can help you get a job abroad.

In *Britain* you could ask for the 'Euroadviser.' Or for someone "*who deals with jobs abroad*" — and the Jobcentre is also where you could find out about work permits and visas if you come from the *United States* — or anywhere else outside one of these European countries — for example if you are studying in an EU country and you want to find out more about work.

Again, you can start off with some general information and then narrow it down — moving from an 'extensive' to an 'intensive' approach, to find out what you want to know

2. Business contacts (2.12). Another network of contacts you can make is for business. Contact that country's joint *Chamber of Commerce* where you are — to find out about companies that trade in both places, or your country's organizations which have an office there. Or your own local or national chamber of commerce, or business advice centre.

In universities there may be somewhere like this as well. *Rotary clubs* — which are associations usually of business people — also have some similar international contacts. What connections or recommendations do they have for scholarships, internships or work placements?

They may also have information about the recognition of qualifications, or trade associations. If you are interested in translation, for translation agencies, for the law, lawyers, and so on

Chambers of Commerce 2.13

There is also a national Chamber of Commerce in that country; and local ones for the place or places you are going, which are worth contacting. (Again, you need to get these addresses and then make your specific inquiry; and to be efficient and organized when you are doing it — by getting the address or number to fax or e-mail and sending one of these — but not be in too much of a hurry. Another approach which doesn't work too well is to send letters with lots of spelling mistakes, or requests which are unclear).

British-American Chamber of Commerce (New York), 52 Vanderbilt Ave, New York, NY 10017, *USA*; tel 212-661-4060; fax 212-661-4074 (the country code for America is '1'); in San Francisco: 415-296-8645; fax 415-296-9649; in the *UK*, tel 0207-404 6400; fax 0207-404 6828

In *France*, the *Franco-British Chamber of Commerce and Industry* can give information about business: 31 rue Boissy d'Anglas, 75008, Paris

In *Greece*, the *British Hellenic Chamber of Commerce* has a list of companies there: 25 Vas Sofia Ave, 106 74, Athens; tel +1-7210361; fax +1-7218751 (country code 30 plus this number). Try 'Greece+your own country name+Chamber of Commerce' as a way to get there on your Internet index or search engine . . .

In *Britain*, the *British-Polish Chamber of Commerce* is 238 – 246 King Street, London W6 ORF; tel 0208-563 7311; fax 0208-563 7299 — no '0' if you dial from outside the *UK*, as often but not always with international telephone codes — the code for Britain being 44. Incidentally, the international code for dialing **out** of a country is very often 00 + country code + area and local code . . .

In *Portugal*, this is the *British-Portuguese Chamber of Commerce* at Rua da Estrela 8, Lisbon; tel +1-396-15-86; fax +1-390-15-13 (country code 351)

The *British-Swedish Chamber of Commerce* in *Sweden* is at: Box 5501, S-11485, Stockhölm; tel +8-783 8204; fax 8-665 0935; or at *www.swednet.uk.org* — like national trade organizations everywhere they now have their website too

British Chambers of Business in Southern Africa (SABRITA), PO Box 103929, Johannesburg 2000, *South Africa,* tel +11-482-4807; fax +11-482-5076 (country code 22)

In *Switzerland*, contact the *British-Swiss Chamber of Commerce* at 155 Freiestrasse, CH-8032 Zürich; tel 1-422 31 31; fax +1-41-1-422 32 44 for more details of trade between the two countries and UK companies with operations there

British Chamber of Commerce in Turkey, Ragip Gymrs Tala, Jad 84, Eminönö, Istanbul 4378, *Turkey*; tel 212-511-41-50; fax 212-513-15-65 (international code 90). It publishes a 'trade journal in English,' 'trade journal in Turkish,' 'Trade Fairs and Exhibitions in Turkey,' and 'Hints to Businessmen in Turkey' for example . . .

And so on.

The Internet is one way, but not the only one, to track down this kind of information. For example, you could find in your local library the equivalent of the *Directory of British Associations* — which has many joint Chambers of Commerce for the *UK*, and abroad — also cultural associations and professional and trade and other societies: *CBD Research Ltd*, 15 Wickham Road, Beckenham, Kent BR3 5JS, UK; tel 0208-650 7745; e-mail cbdresearch @compuserve.com. And business libraries are a good source of information like this. See 2.38

You can find out about many more of these joint chambers of commerce — also for regions like Latin America or Africa — quite

easily; and you could also contact those of other countries — like the British *ones mentioned above, or for the* United States — *which may be very good sources of information for you*

And possible jobs. And keep a file or record of information of what you do

Different languages and areas of influence 2.14

Speaking the language — or going to a country speaking one of these languages — might be reasons for contacting *Portuguese*, or *French*, or *Spanish* companies. For Africa, Latin America, Eastern Europe — wherever the language extends. *German* is spoken quite widely in Eastern Europe; and in the Americas, the *United States* has a strong economic influence; in East Asia, *China* or *Japan*.

Chambre de Commerce is French for Chamber of Commerce; *Cámara de Comercio* in Spanish; or *Industrie-und-Handels-Kammer* is a 'Chamber of Trade and Industry' in German.

When you go to a country you can also consider contacts in other countries which are influential there, and perhaps speak the same language

2.15

3. Newspapers. Newspapers in the country will probably run ads for people speaking different languages, or aimed at more international people — so find out what the local recruitment or jobs publications are.

If you are visiting, look in at a local newsagent and ask — even if you can't speak the language you would be surprised that this kind of publication will be quite easy to find; and quite useful. Some of the advertisements may even be in your own language, for English teachers maybe in English, and so on, even in foreign-language or local-language publications.

Although these might seem far away, the local employers — especially in more 'high-risk' areas where your own job search is likely to be focused — know these ones best. So, it is logical for them to advertise here — even in shop windows, local free publications and on a very local scale — even for jobs which are more international in nature.

These local publications are ways to find out about local, national and international jobs, and where your chances of success are going to be highest

Advertising yourself 2.16

One aim can be to get the news out that you are there, at a certain time and in a certain place. So a small ad in a local community or expatriate publication might be a good idea.

Or similar card sent to organizations like this, or your local church / religious organization there — marked 'for your noticeboard' — or to a cultural organization like the *British Council* (even if you are not British — UK tel 0161-957 7755 to ask where to find a list of their offices abroad) addressed to their 'Library,' or 'Resource Centre,' with a request to display this card where people might see it.

Or to any similar cultural organization you know; or anyone who is there who might put up a notice for you in local shops, newsagents . . . or could offer their own help and advice.

This is a good way to advertise for English lessons or au pair work for instance. Or try local bookstores, or businesses in the area, It's not a bad idea just to ask for advice

Also see the list of Cultural organizations *in an* 'A — Z of jobs abroad' *in* Working abroad. *And consider also the question of what — really — is a good job for you*

Newspapers and other publications 2.17

There are many other national and international newspapers which can help — locally and in your own country — and not just the ones in your local job or career centre — especially these ones from the place you are going, and in the local language.

Many jobs or situations vacant pages are now on the internet — like the *Daily Telegraph* 'appointments' columns in *Britain* at *www.appointments-plus.co.uk*. Also see the *Overseas Jobs Express* website — ***www.overseasjobs.com*** — where there are links to local as well as national sources of jobs — almost anywhere in the world — see *Direct Contacts* and *Sources of Information* for this and many other useful contacts.

Some would be available by subscription — like *Weekly Journey* — for Japanese people in Britain — and in Japanese: *Japan Journals Ltd*, 93 Newman Street, London W1P 3LE, UK; tel 0207-255 3838; fax 0207-255 3313. Or look at the kind of specialist publication which exists for everything from aviation to zookeeping — or any newspaper or newsletter, magazine or website covering your area of interest.

Your local newsagent is where you may well find many more —

or the reading room of the embassy of that country. Just ring up and go along. The national and specialist newspapers will certainly be there — and you might ask someone — if you visit the embassy — for advice; or if they would be able to point you in the right direction: one place you could start your job search.

One tip, if you want to get hold of one of these expensive international newspapers or magazines — but don't want to subscribe — is to write — or send a fax or e-mail — to their 'Advertising Department,' and ask for a sample copy and their rates — meaning their advertising rates. They almost certainly will send you one.

Also, you can find the two or three publications where you are which are most closely related to what you want to do — the ones which will be most useful for job ads — and which are easiest to get hold of in your area. Actors and entertainers in the *UK* read *The Stage,* for instance. There are many international job ads in the area of hospitality in *Hotel and Caterer* magazine.

Or the main ones for English-language teaching would be, for example: *The Guardian*, the *Times Educational Supplement*, and, maybe, the *Times Higher Education Supplement*.

These would all be useful if you are from another country and looking for work in *Britain or the* United States *too* — *or looking for work anywhere in the world*

Many such national publications have international connections. You could find out about these in your newsagent / news dealer, or the reading room of your local library

4. If you are unemployed . . . 2.18

Contribution based benefit. If you are from *Britain*, or *Ireland*, or any other EU or EEA country — *Norway, Iceland, Liechtenstein* — and you are entitled to what is called in *Britain* contribution-based *Jobseeker's Allowance* — and you are unemployed — this means you have the right to go and to look for work, after four weeks registered unemployment, in any *EU / EEA* country; and get away from it all by looking for work there for a period of up to three months.

You just need to have paid enough *National Insurance* / social security contributions in your country. Tell your own *employment service / Jobcentre* first; and they will tell you what to do. This permission to look for work abroad also means you can have your benefit transferred, and you can receive it there. This applies if you come from anywhere in the European Union / EEA area.

There are two forms you need to know about: the *E303*, which they may well send off to the person who is the liaison officer for the scheme at the other end, at the local job / careers service where you are going; and the *E119* , which is for local healthcare. You need to apply for this before you leave too — not just an *E111*, which is for a temporary visit. It entitles you to the same state medical treatment as the your new neighbours in Provence or Picardy . . . all of which might be better than another round of fruitless jobsearching back home.

And you might prefer to be unemployed — and jobseeking — in sunnier climes. This can happen only once, "in any period of unemployment"

2.19

5. Contacting companies

These might be large or small. And the following applies to other organizations, like charities or recruitment agencies too:

In smaller companies, or working for an individual — even if you are finding out about running a business yourself or freelance work you could do — a recommendation or personal contact — from someone you know, or someone who knows someone — works well. Getting to know people is the place to start.

Only in the larger companies are these roles of recruitment and management split up into separate departments — and you will have to try a different, more formal approach.

These will probably have an ongoing recruitment program, as I have mentioned (or 'programme' as it should be in *Britain*). This is part of the company and its activity. Perhaps they need new, qualified and experienced staff to join at any time of the year.

And this is where having a professional CV or résumé and sending the right letter — or fax, or e-mail — comes in

In either case, for companies large and small, you have to know where you are starting, and where you want to go. Don't just write to everyone; but — like your research on the Internet for example — your jobseeking should be focused on getting to know perhaps two or three different companies or organizations better

Contacts on the spot 2.20

Large and small companies may prefer to employ people locally and advertise there. Why not? This is the trend too, away from jobs in some areas being available internationally — despite developments like the internet. And in a sense, job hunting is becoming more local, even as there are more ways nowadays of advertising jobs around the world.

Somebody local is going to appeal more to an employer than someone living somewhere else, at least for most things — except in certain areas of skills shortage like computing, or for summer jobs for students, or for business consultants — where, for different reasons, there is a market for jobs which is international. And the growth of agencies and intermediaries is another sign — or symptom — of this tendency away from centralized decision-making in companies and organizations.

So you will need to know more about what is happening on the ground, locally, even if you apply to a larger company. The head office you contact may not even know what happens in their outposts in *Antigua* or *Afghanistan* — two admittedly unlikely locations. But the Afghans will.

Contact these subsidiaries and local organizations first of all, not the head office. You'll probably need some contacts on the spot

Small companies 2.21

I would recommend finding out about small companies first — not the huge multinationals — which is a way to beat your jobseeking competition. Time is short, and the longer processes of recruitment need to be circumvented. You have to show you are available, and able to work now — and let the right people know as soon as possible. Find out about smaller companies first.

Through Chambers of Commerce. *Or look in your area of work in the* Yellow Pages. *Or when your job search is an 'on-the-spot' one . . . Or personal contacts*

And if you are telling 'decision-makers' in companies about your abilities and skills, don't forget to mention your availability for work in a certain place at a certain time — and when you might be coming to that country and would be able to meet

Send a clear message, so if a job does come up, the employer / company / organization knows you are available, and can do it

International recruitment agencies 2.22

If and when you get there, you can call some of these agencies too — and go and see them. Some international ones would be based in your country: The *Expat Network Contact Directory*, tel 0208-760 5100; e-mail *expatnetwork@cityscape.co.uk* — is one list of these agencies for jobs around the world — and see *DirectContacts* for some more useful recruitment contacts.

Showing, among other things, that employment is one aspect of the 'globalization' of economies almost everywhere — of culture — and language — and even recruitment is becoming a multi-national affair:

Adecco — Adecco Management and Consulting, Rue de Langallerie 11, Case Postale, 1000 Lausanne 4, Switzerland; tel +41-321-66-66; fax +41-21-321-66-28; 100 Redwood Shores Parkway, Redwood City, CA 94065; USA; tel 650-610-1000; fax 650-610-1076; *www.adecco.com. "The world's leading personnel service —*

3,200 offices throughout the world — staffing over 200,.000 companies in 52 companies." For local and international jobs especially secretarial, industrial, and office work

Antal International Executive Recruitment, 2nd floor, 90 Tottenham Court Road, London W1P 0AN, UK; tel 0207-637 2001; fax 0207-637 0949. Offices in Central and Eastern Europe, China, Latin America and Australasia . . . for managers, IT, accountancy. finance, and consultants for international and local companies; e-mail cv@antal-int.com; *www.antal.com* — *"a global recruitment solution applied locally"*

Arabian Careers Limited, 115 Shaftesbury Avenue, London WC2 8AD, UK; tel 0207-379 7877; fax 0207-379 0385; *www.arabiancareers.com* — specializing in worldwide recruitment for healthcare and training roles in *Saudi Arabia*, including doctors / dentists in general practice, general and speciality nurses / midwives, pharmacists, therapists, technologists, and technicians, administrators and support services

Cannon Persona — part of the biggest recruitment agency in *Japan*: jobs in London and around *Britain:* tel 0207-489 8141; fax 0207-236 5785; *www.cpir.com*; e-mail info@cpir.com

Contracts Consultancy Limited, 162-164 Upper Richmond Road, Putney, London SW15 2SL, UK; tel 0208-333 4141; fax 0208-333 4151; e-mail ccl@ccl.uk.com; *www.ccl.uk.com* — oil and gas

Internet Employment Services, 134a Great Victoria Street, Belfast BT2 7BG, UK; tel 028-9031-2626

Opta Consulting, 4th floor, Artillery House, Artillery Row, Westminster, London SW1P 1RT, UK; tel 0207-222 5204; *www.opta.com* — telecommunications — and strong ties with

France and Germany. They are currently recruiting recruitment people too . . .

Petrolic Consultants Ltd, 174 High Street, Guildford, Surrey GU1 3HW, UK; tel 01483-302133; fax 01483-579891; e-mail petrolic@compuserve.com — architects and quantity surveyors required for civil engineering, building, highway and bridge projects in *Ireland*

PremierPersonnel, 25-29 High Street, Leatherhead, Surrey KT22 8AB, UK; tel 01372-379183; e-mail pjdepremper.demon.co.uk; *www.premierpersonnel.co.uk* — construction in the Middle East and worldwide, electricians and engineers, for public utilities and manufacturing

Robert W. Hort & Associates, Certified Placement Consultants, toll free 1-800-600-4091, e-mail info@CanadaUSemployment.com; 620 Wilson Ave., Suite 225, Toronto, Ontario M3K 1Z3, *Canada*; 3223 3rd Ave South, Suite 200, Seattle, Washington 98134, *USA*; *www.CanadaUSemployment.com.* Also for visa and advice services

Silicon Valley Consultants Ltd, 60 High Street, Sandhurst, Berkshire GU47 8DY, UK; tel 01252-877778; fax 01252-875737; e-mail svg@silicon.valley.co.uk — computing

Thomas Mining Associates, PO Box 2010, Lancing, West Sussex BN15 8HZ, UK; tel 01903-753511; fax 01903-753510; e-mail dennis@thomasmining.prestel.co.uk — mining, engineering and construction

TM International, 36-38 rue des Mathurins, Paris 8iéme, *France*; tel +33-1-47 42 71 00; fax +33-1-47 42 18 87 — secretarial. Source: *The Times* newspaper, *Premier Appointments* and *First Executive* sections, Thursdays. And see similar national newspapers, and 2.15

Towngate Personnel Ltd., 65 Seamoor Road, Westbourne, Bournemouth BH4 9AE, UK; tel 01202-752955; fax 01202-752954 — hotels, cruises and catering jobs

TRC — The Recruitment Consultancy Ltd., 296 Regent Street, London W1R 5HD, UK; tel 0207-436 4424; fax 0207-436 7690; e-mail john@trcltd.demon.co.uk — "*mainly for computing*" they say

www.netjobs.com is one example of a commercial agency on the internet

www.overseasjobs.com — is the *Overseas Jobs Express* website once again

The *Federation of Recruitment and Employment Service* (otherwise known as *FRES*) is also worth calling to ask about a particular job area and agencies for this. It is an association of employment agencies: tel 0207-323 4300; freephone 0800-320588 36-38 Mortimer Street, London W1N 7RB, *UK; www.fres.co.uk;* e-mail info@fres.co.uk.

They can send a list of members offering jobs overseas, or of agencies offering work in particular areas, like 'linguists and translation,' for a small fee, payable by credit card over the phone.

They sent me a list of about 200 translation agencies taken from their directory of members for instance; or you might find this kind of association in other countries.

There are probably similar associations of recruitment agencies and consultants where you are going, and private and public organizations offering career advice

Contacting decision-makers 2.23

Make your approach friendly, but also well-organized, business-like . . . And sometimes you will need to send your letters off not to recruiters and recruitment agencies but to different decision-makers there, the people who can help you 'make friends and influence people.' If you don't know any, start at the top and write to 'The Director.' Find out a name if you can.

Perhaps the job involves speaking a foreign language? Then the letter can be translated into the local one — or maybe send two versions of the same letter. Make it neat and clear

A 'case history' 2.24

You should be realistic; and only apply for jobs you believe you can do. But use your imagination too. And think about things using some lateral thinking.

An example — if you were looking for secretarial work or for a work placement / internship in another country and were interested in politics — and if you had the right experience and foreign language / secretarial skills — as you would have to — how would you find your way to a job abroad?

You could start by contacting your own local deputy, MP, or senator, in your parliament, house of representatives, senate . . . and ask for a contact, from the person representing you, there.

They could then put you in touch with their opposite number in the place you are going. In Brussels it might be an MEP in the European Parliament, who you could end up working for. Or in Washington, Paris, Tokyo . . .

Begin locally. You might then apply to someone you have found through one of these local contacts and connections, who you have been put in touch with — even with some kind of recommendation from the person you originally contacted . . .

And there are people all over the world like this — in trade and commerce, charitable organizations, and international companies, in fact in many fields, who have connections abroad; and can point you in the right direction. Think about this.

And many companies, charities, universities also employ administrators, and professional secretarial staff, as well as some volunteers and interns — who might take on someone they have been introduced to in this way.

Sometimes there is a 'getting-to-know-you' period before you get a job, too, when you are making contacts — and making yourself known to people who might employ you. You need to know more about the world of work you may eventually enter, getting to know how things are.

At this stage it is reasonable to contact not just one person, but several in the area you are interested in.

Almost any local contact could lead you to a job abroad, in almost any field, if you follow it up this way, using just a little imagination

And it would almost certainly be more effective from your point of view to apply for a job this way than applying to the bureaucracy or civil service in that country, for instance; or even sending off piles of letters to job agencies, which will have priorities which are different from simply getting you a job — you could say that the aim of the job agency is to provide recruits for employers, not jobs for people — they are not always the right place to go first of all

And you really can consider getting an international job with a contact which starts off in your own country — not necessarily like the example above, but by going about it your own way

Also, you don't have to follow up each contact — or possible job — one after another but you can follow many at the same time

The main point is, don't be afraid to try a different approach

A job offer 2.25

But of course there are many difficulties on the way.

If there weren't, everybody would also be following the same route to the same destination; but life is really full of many ways of getting to your goal; and goals which change *en route*.

There is something else to consider — in fact three main points — when you reach the end of this process — and especially if your job search has been difficult and you feel the need to take your chance when finally it comes and an offer has been made . . . which is the time just to step back for a moment to think about the situation, where you are now and where you are going.

These are three main points **ambiguity**; **exploitation**; and **suitability**.

Is this job really right? Will it really do what you want it to do? Is it really where you want to be? Is it what you thought it was?

And think about the job offer which has been made; and not just assume it is what you wanted, or wished for. And you can consider your personal relations with colleagues, the contract, and what the job itself involves.

These are questions which apply to working anywhere; and doing anything, more or less. And every language has a phrase which goes something like 'All that glitters is not gold' — for good reason. Life moves on — and even an opportunity missed won't look as bad six months down the line.

And I would say, don't make too much of a sacrifice for a job which seems — but only seems — like your dream.

The three points to consider:

1. ***Ambiguity*** *— A job offer which is ambiguous, or a long time in the future, is really no good. Is the job offer which has been made clear? Will there be more demands later on?*

2. ***Exploitation*** *— Of course you may be ready to work long hours for little pay, but think about this not only from a money point of view; but also how this will affect your relations with your employer — what they think of you — and exactly what your future in the job is — and your personal relations with colleagues.*

Exploitation is not just a money or 'hard-work' question; but is really about human relations

3. ***Suitability*** *— The job should be clear and unambiguous, but also suitable. Look at the contract — and look at the job*

IN THE MOVIE OF 'THE BEACH' THE LEONARDO DICAPRIO CHARACTER FINDS HIMSELF IN THE JUNGLE, WONDERING HOW HE GOT THERE, SURROUNDED BY PEOPLE HE DOES NOT KNOW, IN CIRCUMSTANCES HE WOULD RATHER ESCAPE. HE LITERALLY DOESN'T THINK BEFORE HE TAKES THE PLUNGE . . . A WARNING MAYBE NOT TO DO THE SAME!

Other contacts and connections 2.26

Your international circle of connections and friends will grow if you really do end up living and working abroad. This is another advantage of living and working in another country — which could lead to new opportunities later on.

Then there are all the more formal ways of jobsearching which are mentioned here, getting hold of a local *Yellow Pages* or business directory, the bilateral chamber of commerce, professional or trade associations, or other direct contacts.

But jobsearching is really about people. If you can explain your predicament to someone there who can help, this holds out much more hope than even a very sympathetic careers adviser or colleague who doesn't really know the place — or just having a list of any old names and addresses . . .

Think of all the international connections which you can start with already — people you already know

The right contacts 2.27

There are all kinds of countries and companies out there, all kinds of organizations, and ways of doing things. Contacts and connections sometimes work differently in different countries. Sometimes, some will be OK; and others, it will not be the right time to say, "*Well, the last time I was chatting to Tony Blair he recommended your dynamic organization as a possible business partner for myself . . ."*

Come to think of it, the political approach may always be the wrong one. Since the last time you were there, the people who were in power are now in prison, and the hardliners have taken over. A risky approach.

One point is that people in positions of power and influence, working in companies or politics — everywhere — who have already achieved some kind of importance — have learned to tell the difference between a real connection — with somebody they know, whom you may also know — or if it is just a business card you have or name you are dropping (or vica versa) — in other words if your own connections or letters of recommendation count or not.

They can usually tell the difference between a VIP and a VUP (a Very Unimportant Person)

VIPs and VUPs 2.28

But in some places, which are only now entering the modern era — or have been excluded from it by their history, or economic circumstances — it is really the VIPs you need to contact if it is work in their company / area of influence that you want — or to do business there, and to try the personal approach.

This might be more important in some countries than in other, more 'modern' places.

Where they might not know if you are a VIP or a VUP yourself. They might still be operating according to the old rules — when status really was the badge you wore, or a place you had been assigned, or a business card you had . . . And the whole process of making friends and influencing people was much more formal. In many countries, you really do need connections like this — or a name to drop.

And these things — as I have mentioned — in business and work — really do operate differently in different places.

This could be an advantage or a disadvantage, depending on your point of view, and how sensitive you are to such nuances; and if you have an international outlook — one where you believe that cultures may be different but people are basically the same — and if you are open to new ways of doing things. This is another important part of living and working in a different country. And leaving your prejudices behind.

For the business-minded, if you go to a really distant destination — where few of your compatriots are living — there may also be more opportunities for work and business there

International jobs 2.29

It is not true to say that all 'international' jobs are advertised internationally. And the idea that you can get a job with one organization — except in some areas like diplomacy or the army — and then continue your international career, is not always helpful.

Nowadays your career is much more likely to be seen as coming from you, not from outside — the decisions which you make about your life — and your own future. It is <u>your</u> career

6. Colleges and universities 2.30

Where you could find your way to an international career even if you are not studying at college or university. And their student-run employment offices and noticeboards can a good source of jobs and information for everyone — see 2.41 — about jobs in tourism for instance.

Graduate careers 2.31

Milkround Online is the "*web site for graduate recruitment*" and for students looking for a job, with company information on, they say, hundreds of potential employers; and many other services: *www.milkround.co.uk*. 26 Charlotte Street, London W1P 1HJ, UK, tel 0207-419 5190, fax 0207-209 5056, info@milkround.co.uk: "*Visit our Website today!*"

To find out more about international careers, also look on your college noticeboard, or go to the employment or careers office. These can be good places to go for anyone looking for a job abroad, not just college students

A gap year 2.32

College noticeboards and employment offices offer lots of advice — and have lots to advise about: grape-picking in *France*, pea-picking in *Australia*, au pairing in *America*, or joining the thousands of others saving the *Costa Rican* rainforest.

Some leaflets and books are produced by the 'Central Bureau for Educational Visits and Exchanges' — 10 Spring Gardens, London SW1A 2BN, UK, tel 0207-389 4004 — part of the *British Council* (same address) and usually known more briefy as the *Central Bureau*. 'Ten Ways to Work and Travel' suggests looking after children, tourism, working in hospitality, the aforementioned fruitpicking, leading groups on tours, being an instructor — for example for teaching English — archaeological work — once described to me as digging a hole and filling it in again — and volunteering — or staying at home. In fact, earning some money first, and then setting off, may be the best way. Is this a holiday . . . or a job (a question which the members of the international workcamp in 'The Beach' have not answered)?

Organizations cited include the *CCIVS — Coordinating Committee for International·Voluntary Service* — UK office tel 01206-298215 — for projects working for up to a month with young people. See *DirectContacts.* Or the *Council on International Exchange*, 205 East 42nd Street, New York, NY 10017-5706, USA, *www.councilexchanges.org*, also has a long history organizing exchanges and study / work experience programs for young people interested in education, work or travel, from *Australia* to *Japan.*

The Central Bureau *publishes two other information sheets similar to the above: 'Ten Ways to Fill the Gap' and 'Ten Ways to Discover the World' —free on receipt of an SAE (stamped addressed envelope — or a self-addressed envelope with* International Reply Coupons / IRCs *to the correct amount. And they sent me their leaflet on* Working in another country of the European Union

Letters abroad 2.33

There are many forms of writing and scripts around the world. But the roman, or 'English' one is understood by people almost everywhere. If you use this you should follow the format of a usual *British / United States* letter — with the name, then street, then town and zip code / postcode and country. This is OK everywhere.

Otherwise, in Eastern Europe and Asia, usually the country is at the top, going down to the name of the person at the bottom — so you could write the country name twice — once at the top — in the local language if you are following this way of doing things — with the country name again at the bottom in your own language / roman letters, too, for your own local postman or lady.

Your own address — if it needs to be returned — should be written on the back flap of the envelope — a practice which is falling into disuse in *Britain*, but which continues abroad. Air mail stickers are needed — or write the words 'AIR MAIL — PAR AVION', which is fine — and air-mail envelopes or aerogramme letters are lighter.

Hola! *is the Royal Mail's International Pen Pal Club in* Britain — *for children and teenagers. You can request a leaflet from the Royal Mail — Hola!, Royal Mail, Department 3001, FREEPOST NEA 3981, Hendon Road, Sunderland SR9 9YE, UK (FREEPOST meaning you don't need a stamp in Britain — this is a bit like a freephone or toll-free telephone number, only accessible inside the country). There is a £7.50 fee plus an extra £1.50 for each new Pen Pal you require.* "And a card to fill in, then you send it back and you are a member." *See Chapter 5 for more on the post office and its services —* 5.30

Rejection letters 2.34

Have you read the job advertisements in your local paper lately? How many will be filled by someone who already knows someone? Or is there already some preconceived idea about the kind of person they want? (The words 'young', 'enthusiastic' and 'good sense of humour' spring to mind — and watch out especially for 'Do you enjoy working as part of a busy team?')

Is there already someone — I sometimes wonder — who they had in mind to do the job but maybe they had to advertise it anyway? Recruitment is not like the 'X-Files' — or is it? Isn't it just a little strange — if you have been looking at job ads over a long period — how some seem to come up again and again?

What can this tell you? First of all not to be too taken aback when you get the standard rejection letter, telling you the quality of the applicants was so high etc., and they hope you will find something more suitable in future — when you applied in the first place because you thought you ***were*** a good person to do the job.

Often these are totally unrelated to what you said on the phone, or in your letter. But there is no reason to be discouraged. These are just standard rejection letters

Mysterious vacancies 2.35

Sometimes jobs advertised — in true Mulder and Scully fashion — do not even exist. Or they have already been filled, and this is just a repeat advertisement. The organization has to advertise it, anyway, because officially it must — but already it has someone in mind for the job. I have worked out finally — after many years — that jobs at the BBC are like this.

But yours could — and perhaps should — be a more high-risk approach — because jobs which are higher on the risk scale are much easier to get, at least to start off with: A more 'creative' approach is best for a business opportunity, or some freelance work, or going to get a job abroad when you have to do this in a hurry . . .

Be prepared to try an unorthodox approach — like writing off to relevant vacancies which were advertised in publications this time last year. The cycle of work — and recruitment — is often annual. A job is out there . . .

Just ringing up is never a bad idea when you don't quite know what the job involves — especially if you have a contact or name for someone. Or you might send a fax or e-mail — even by mobile phone; and already video phones — through your computer — and videoconferencing — even video interviews — no longer a thing of some science-fiction future but the everyday present, making the world seem a smaller place . . .

Phonecards 2.36

Available to almost everyone are international phonecards, which offer much cheaper international rates for telephone calls, and faxes. They are a very useful thing to have. On the table in front of me is an 'anywhere, anytime discount card' produced by *WorldXChange Communications*, with a UK Customer Assistance number: tel 0207-987 4000. Small shops and newsstands are often where these are sold.

7. Libraries and information services 2.37

Maybe you found this book in one. Libraries — even local ones — can be good sources of information about companies, jobs, careers and travel.

Business libraries 2.38

One example of a business library is the *Department of Trade and Industry* library in London — otherwise known as 'EMIC' —

where students and researchers can book an appointment (Kingsgate House, 66-74 Victoria Street, London SW1E 6SW, UK; tel 0207-215 5444 — open until 8pm weekdays). A call may get you through to a queueing system — then you press '0', or wait to get through to a member of staff.

The largest in *Britain* is the *British Library*, which has an information service for business — see 2.39 — where they would even do the research work for you — for which they would also charge a fee. On the internet, you might find your way to *www.bl.uk* where the main catalogue is searchable online.

Your ministry for the economy or trade may have its own library too

General libraries 2.39

The *Westminster Central Reference Library*, St. Martin's Street, London WC2H 7HP, UK — is one place to find foreign telephone directories in Central London, as I remember, just off Trafalgar Square. Many local and business libraries have them too. This one has "*half a million books, magazines and information souces in stock.*"

And the internet is like a library . . . with many many sources of reference; and routes you can take through to almost any information on earth. Some reference sources to begin with are: *www.eb.com* (the *Encyclopedia Britannica*); *www.mth.uea.ac.uk/VL* — meaning the *Virtual Library* — where you might well begin: a university site geared towards scholars and academics, but with areas like business and economics also covered. Or go — if you have access to this method of research — which can be the beginning but should never be the end of your enquiries — to the *Library of Congress* at *lcweb.loc.gov/homepage.*

And if not, you can always visit, or write: *The Library of Congress,* 101 Independence Ave. S.E., Washington, D.C. 20540, *U.S.A.* — or telephone: 202-707-5000.

In *Britain,* you could also contact the *British Library* Science Technology and Business department and information service — *STB* — for a professional research service on any aspect of business and technology: tel 0207-7288/7494/7496. Their rates will suit larger companies rather than individuals — this is a commercial service. Or *English Contacts Abroad* — see the *Direct Contacts* section. Also, the *British Library / Lloyds-TSB Business Line* — a"*quick*" enquiry telephone service, which can find out such things as key company, product and similar information, as well — it says in their handout — as "*Overseas contacts, assistance in identifying useful companies and organizations overseas.*"

Research can — and should — be something you can do yourself however — in local libraries as well as business and national ones — and is much more useful that way.

You can find some more Websites — *useful starting-points for any internet search about travel or employment — on the back page*

The USA 2.40

In the *USA,* you might call the *Federal Trade Commission Library,* 6th Street and Pennsylvania Avenue, NW, Washington, DC 20580 on 202-236-2395; or the *Library of Congress* also has an 'Information Office' on 202-287-5108 — see 2.39.

Trade and business libraries like these are good places to go for lists of companies, those with dealings or operations there, contacts for local chambers of commerce, trade associations, Yellow Pages, *and business telephone directories, or just about anything*

Universities and cultural institutes 2.41

Or contact the relevant embassy — where sometimes a resource centre or cultural institute will be. Or call a local university, and their department of French, or Spanish, or whatever . . . and they will know where a similar association or institute might be there, or where to get in touch.

These could let you know about local societies and organizations interested in that country — also see *Sources of Information*. In your locality, universities and colleges can be a very good source, once again, not only the faculty or department for the language, for business, or for some other subject area — or the careers centre for example — but also there may be a student-run employment office for example.

An obvious idea when you are studying there; but not so obvious if you have not been to college, or are just living in the neighbourhood

Your international job search 2.42

Begins by finding out more about the destination, especially its capital city, where the head offices of many organizations / companies, as well as government agencies will be. Or look in the local phone book — which may be your most direct link before you get there — under 'language schools' for English teaching, or in the relevant section, engineering, local shops or stores, or for any area of work — and in the local newspapers too — and all the other routes to getting a job abroad mentioned in this chapter.

But most of all it begins with you. Having your own interests and an international outlook are a good starting-point

A summary 2.43

Your aim — if you are trying to get a job — in a certain field, a certain line of work, with a certain ability you have — a job you can do, or one you have done before — anywhere in the world — is to be:

the right person, in the right place, at the right time

Key Points

You can work almost anywhere in the world, and in almost any field, if you have the right qualifications and experience

Some areas, like language teaching, or work in tourism — dealing with people from your own country — will be open to people who can't speak the language well

Find out about visas and residence and work permits from the embassy / consulate

Often work will be restricted to highly qualified professional people — or those with enough capital to start a business. Contact the consulate or embassy first, not a visa or relocation agency — also for information about companies

3

Getting there

"However far you go, you will never leave yourself behind . . ."

Your time leading up to your decision to get a job or go and live abroad doesn't need to become too complex or difficult, just requiring a little thought.

This applies to all your travel and moving arrangements too. All you need is to give yourself enough time.

A useful leaflet produced by 'World Service Enquiry' — a part of the charity *Christians Abroad* — 1 Stockwell Green, London SW9 9HP, UK; tel 0207-737 7811; fax 0207-737 3237 — recommends you take some time out before you wait for your work to start to make these arrangements. "*You need to allow time for visas and vaccinations. Many organizations recruit continually, others once, or twice a year. Find out as much as possible about the organization before committing yourself, and don't burn your bridges until you have your travel ticket!*"

Before you go 3.1

The *Careers Europe Database of Careers Information* — otherwise known as '*Exodus*' — says there are certain questions which you

— or a careers adviser — should consider before you go (for any trip — for business or pleasure — anywhere in the world):

1. *Do you speak the language?*
2. *Do you know anything about the culture of the country?*
3. *Do you have somewhere to stay?*
4. *Do you have enough money to live on?*
5. *If you want to come home, do you have enough for the fare?*
6. *Do you have a passport? What other documents do you need?*
7. *Do you have suitable insurance cover? How about health?*

This useful database — with documents on everything from A Guide to EU Organizations *to study in different countries to employment and careers agencies, and advice for specific careers and jobs you can do, in the EU and beyond — is produced by* Careers Europe *— and also see the* Living abroad *chapter*

Do's and Don'ts of travelling abroad 3.2

Before you go on your trip abroad, some research will help you avoid some potentially serious problems. One place to contact is your own *Foreign Ministry* which — like the *UK Foreign and Commonwealth Office*, may have advice for its own nationals going abroad. The following is from the *Travel Advice* they issue:

"FCO Travel Advice is designed to help British Travellers avoid trouble by providing succinct and up-to-date information on threats

to personal safety arising from political unrest, lawlessness, violence, natural disasters, epidemics, anti-British demonstrations and aircraft safety."

"Over 1,000 notices have been issued annually in recent years covering more than 140 countries. Notices are constantly reviewed on the basis of information from our posts overseas."

"The public can obtain Travel Advice Notices *by telephoning the Travel Advice Unit direct between 09.30 and 16.00 hours Monday to Friday on 0207-238 4503/4 or by faxing on 0207-238 4545 or by writing to the above address. They are supplemented by "Do's and Don'ts" leaflets for 25 countries"* — mainly for those with large numbers of UK visitors.

"The full range of notices is also available on BBC2 Ceefax *page 470 onwards, on the FCO's World Wide Web server on the Internet under Consular and Visa Services, along with a range of Consular Division publicity material. The address is http://www.fco.gov.uk/"*

"These are distributed throughout the travel industry. The Federation of Tour Operators, *the* Association of British Travel Agents *and the* Association of Independent Tour Operators *also distribute notices to their respective memberships. More than 90% of the travel industry can access this information."*

In the USA, *you can contact the* Centers for Disease Control and Prevention, *1600 Clifton Road, Atlanta, GA 30333, tel 404-639-3311, toll-free fax 888-232-3299, www.cdc.gov/travel — information on 'Destinations,' Reference materials,' 'Outbreaks,' Traveling with Children,' 'Special Needs Travelers,' 'Safe Food and Water,' 'Vaccinations,' even 'Cruise Ships' — or the* State Department

Travel advice 3.3

The UK — like American and other governments — also produce country-by-country updates for destinations where visitors are thought to be at risk. For example, at the time of writing, their advice for travel to *Somalia* is: "*Many parts of Somalia remain insecure. We advise against travel to southern Somalia. The north-west is generally stable, but the situation could change without warning . . . There is no British representation in Somalia.*" For *Macedonia*, they say that "*there is an acute shortage of hotel accommodation in Skopje. Visitors should ensure they have accommodation booked before travelling . . .*" And for *Tajikistan*, succinctly, they say: "*We strongly advise against all travel to Tajikistan until further notice.*"

Other *Consular Services* information leaflets, including 'Checklist for Travellers', 'Backpackers and Independent Travellers', and 'British Consular Services Abroad', are widely distributed through travel agents, airlines and airports, public libraries and *Citizens Advice Bureaux*. Bulk supplies can be obtained by faxing their 'Distribution Centre' on 01444-246620. (The *FCO* also strongly recommends that all travellers abroad take out adequate comprehensive insurance — and for medical and innoculation advice, contact their doctor).

"*Visa information is available from the relevant Embassy/ Consulate in London*"

Local laws and customs 3.4

What kind of advice can you get from the *Foreign Office* (or your own national Foreign Ministry)? Some of these 'travel advice notices' might err on the side of caution: but you are strongly recommended to contact your own *Foreign Ministry* before any trip to one of the more unsafe areas of the world, like the *U.S. Department of State*, Washington, DC, 20520 (postal address); tel 202-647-4000; *www.state.gov*. Not that Washington is unsafe of course.

The British FCO's *Do's and Don'ts in Turkey* tells you to *"respect local laws and customs."* For example, *"it is an offence to insult the Turkish nation or the national flag, or to deface or tear up currency."* Also, *"don't take photographs of or near military or other official installations . . ."*

For *Sri Lanka*, we are told about local sensibilities in dress and other matters — see below — and warned about the civil war in (mainly) the north of the country; to take care of things like passports and valuables; or arriving without a licence or going there without medical insurance.

These travel advice leaflets are widely distributed in places like post offices, through airlines and airports, or public libraries and — in the UK — Citizens Advice Bureaux

For more about the advice issued about specific destinations, also see the FCO *internet site:* www.fco.gov.uk/

Religion 3.5

An awareness of religious sensibilities will be important in many places. You may disgree with some aspects of the local religion / religions — but remember that where you come from you would have your own sensitivities too, religious or otherwise. These should be respected.

It is one of the paradoxes of modern travel that, moving to another country, we can come into close contact with a more religious sensibility for the first time — when we may not have thought about this much at home — and in this way globalization can actually promote the particularities of local culture and religion.

Perhaps this is why many people today to adopt a religion which is not their own, or which originated somewhere else.

Somehow, this goes with the experience of foreign travel too. In the past — and even today in many places — there is a kind of travel for religious or spiritual purposes which may be only half realized but which marks many experiences of going to live or stay in another country

Photos 3.6

If you think about it, offence can be caused by taking photos without permission — anywhere. Unless you are a professional, it is best to ask permission, or at least seek this from people you wish to photograph, with a smile perhaps. Also, by dressing immodestly — and this applies to men and women — you can cause grave offence, and great difficulty for yourself. In its *Sri Lanka* leaflet, the British Foreign Office says you should *"bear in mind religious sensibilities. You should not enter a Buddhist temple wearing headgear or with bare legs."*

You may be on 'The Beach.' *You don't have to live it . . .*

Clothes 3.7

Especially when you are going to live and work there, you should bring neat, work-style clothes with you, or a suit — which will be useful almost anywhere — when you are travelling and when you are working too.

More casual clothes might mark you off as a 'hippy', or a tourist, and maybe give the wrong impression in the workplace too

Drugs 3.8

Mind you, those strong pastel colours are in fashion. And finally, *"don't get involved with drugs."* Which would apply anywhere; and this would include the casual use of soft drugs which may cause offence to locals — just as it would in your own country — and places like *India* and *Nepal* are not any more marijuana-friendly than anywhere else, although you may see drugs smoked in beachside bars and restaurants.

Apart from the law — which may be stricter than you think — the locals will look down on this kind of public behaviour

Getting your ticket 3.9

This involves checking all the best sources of information, in newspapers, travel agencies, or on the internet — and also on the *BBC Ceefax* service, and other 'interactive' TV services.

A good travel agency is the place to start, one which really knows the place. They can advise you about many aspects of your trip. You might check with a small or independent one first, specializing in that country. Where you might get a more personal service — and many travel agencies, large and small, also offer services for work / business travellers and those travelling with — or for — their companies.

Find out about these independent or local travel agencies / tour operators from the tourist office. Many will be based there — the national tourist offices will be able to tell you about these — and some would have offices in your country, or connections in both places

Business or discount tickets? 3.10

Business travel sometimes means booking business class — which is not usually the most cost-effective way, or even the best. The travel pages of the national newspapers are where you find the bargains and special offers, and travel agencies or 'bucket shops' which can usually sell air tickets at a discount, nearly always at a much lower price than the airlines. You can call some of these.

But it is a myth that tickets bought from agents will be less flexible than those bought from the airlines. Discount ticket sellers are almost always best for a cheap long-haul flight

Special offers and low-cost airlines 3.11

Check the windows of travel agencies — and newspapers too — for other deals and special offers. Remember, some of the larger travel agency chains may only work with certain airlines, so check one or two to get an idea.

Within Europe or the *United States*, the best deals will often be with the low-cost airlines, like *Ryanair* in *Ireland*, *EasyJet*, and *Go* in the *UK*. *Buzz* is presently based in the *Netherlands* — and more and more of these low-cost routes from *Ireland* to *Greece* are springing up — as well as in the *United States*, where they began. But for the long haul, agencies can usually provide a better deal.

British Midland: 0870-240 7041

buzz: 0870-240 7070; *www.buzzaway.com*

easyJet (London Luton, Gatwick and Stanstead, Liverpool, Glasgow etc): 0870-6000 000; *www.easyJet.com*

go (the British-Airways owned rival to the above): 0845-6054 321; *www.go-fly.com*

KLM uk (worldwide network): 08705-074074; *www.klm.uk.com*

ryanair (pioneering Irish low-cost airline): 0870-156 8569; *www.ryanair.ie*

TAP Air Portugal: UK 0845-6010932 *(information and reservations); or* 020-87452044; *Portugal:* 01-841 6644 — *telephone check-in*

Travelbag (agency — business travel team): 0870-730 0081; *www.travelbag.co.uk*

Flightbookers (agency): www.flightbookers.net or *ebookers.com*

Ticket restrictions 3.12

Your ticket may have some restrictions which means you can't cancel — so don't book this kind of flight if you haven't made up your mind. How flexible is the fare? This is a question which the airline could answer, as well as the agency. This applies to tickets from the cut-price ticket agencies; and discounted tickets sold by the airline.

An open return or round-trip ticket means you can return any time. And if you do have to change the date, it may be that you can do this also with many other kinds of tickets, perhaps by paying a supplement — even for some low-price student fares. You can always ask.

It depends on the category of the ticket — and there can be quite a few of these, which vary from airline to airline, and route to route. Call the airline — and also preferably a day or two before departure check on your flight.

Pay with your credit card . . . as some provide their own travel insurance, for you and your family ("*not a substitute for your normal travel and medical insurance,*" they say).

You are looking for the best deal — for you, and maybe also your family — which would mean asking about children's seats; which might be half-price or less, or for very young children, even free. There may be a special offer — like one currently for travel with *Eurostar* (the Channel Tunnel train service) from London to Paris, Lille or Brussels, where children under 16 go free.

Eurostar: 0870-518 6186; *www.eurostar.com*

Eurotunnel: 0870-538 8388; *www.eurotunnel.com*

Children 3.13

Getting there with a family also means taking account of the needs of each family member, and getting your children involved. Perhaps you can find a way to visit in advance. They can keep a diary of their new life there too — or the journey — or the move — and find out more about the country they are going to.

Schools could help here: by keeping in touch with their pupils who move away. Children have a lot to leave behind when moving abroad — something they will not necessarily want to do. Others will be more enthusiastic about the change.

Whichever way it goes, this is a situation which will not necessarily be eased by sending them to a private or special international school — which also means moving — for them — or separation from their parents and friends; and losing out on advantages like the adventure of being in a foreign country, or the challenge — which they may find easier than you — of learning a new language.

Some may disagree. But there is never quite a 'quick fix' for your children's education, even assuming you can afford one. This will only suit some circumstances

ECIS *is the* European Council of International Schools: UK *tel 01730-268244; fax 01730-267914; e-mail ecis@ecis.org; http://* www.ecis.org; the Americas *tel +1-908-903-0552; fax +1-908-580-9381; e-mail malyecisna@aol.com;* Iberia *tel +34-1-562-6722; fax +34-1-563-6854; e-mail 06500.3325@compuserve.com;* Australasia *tel +61-3-5781-1351; fax +61-3-5781-1151; e-mail intedcon-@ontherun.com.au*

Your child's point of view 3.14

A letter highlighting some of these issues appeared in the problem page of the 'Mirror' newspaper in *Britain* recently, about a twelve-year old girl moving to *Ireland*. Her parents were going there to work.

They were sent tips by readers about all the positive advantages of the move: to "*go and visit the school*"; and how to make new friends — and that it wasn't so far away after all — and also on the importance of keeping in touch with friends and family at home.

This can still be a painful process, though. Some correspondents offered advice recommending making a 'deal' that she could return at 16 if she wasn't happy. Listening sympathetically will also be important — and it was recommended you try to find some interesting things for your children to look forward to when you get there. Or speak to someone else who has already been to the country.

Many will enjoy the adventure: and not want to miss out. But perhaps it is a good idea also to make it clear that you have to go — if you do — and not encourage any false hopes. And not worry too much about a new language, a new school . . . Children, and especially young ones, will probably adapt more easily than you think.

Among the services offered by Corona Worldwide — *also see* Living abroad — *are 'Contacts Overseas for Women', '. . . for Men', '. . . on Returning to the UK', and a 'Dependents' Escort Service' — "meeting and escorting children and elderly travellers from train or plane and across London on outward or returning journeys"*

Corona Worldwide (Women's Corona Society): *tel/fax 020-76120-4407; e-mail: hq@coronaww.prestel.co.uk; c/o Commonwealth Institute, Kensington High Street, London W8 6NQ, UK*

Business people 3.15

Are treated like children sometimes, lured on by special offers, exaggerated claims about reclining headrests, or slightly more legroom, or absurd advertising encouraging them to pay over the odds for even short-distance trips. Business travellers tend to be the ones their company is paying for; and will be shopping around in a different way — and mainly concerned about getting there fast, reliably and in comfort.

Long waits in airports are the bane of business travel — and exaggerated ideas about the hell of airports — but minimizing these is one key to arranging a successful business trip.

And when you use a business travel agent, or recommend one for colleagues / staff to use, you should be aware that some of these have their own individual and incentivized deals with airlines as well. They get air miles too . . .

TAP Air Portugal 3.16

"TAP Air Portugal *introduces its new Navigator Class and Navigator Class Brochure. This coincides with the launch of the new Navigator Eurobudget fare which entitles passengers to travel Navigator Business class for the price of an economy (Eurobudget) ticket.*"

"*At just £486 plus tax, passengers flying to Lisbon, Porto or Faro in* Portugal *will automatically fly in Navigator Business class and benefit from exclusive check-in, use of business lounge, superior in-flight service and the opportunity to earn even more Qualiflyer frequent flyer miles . . .*" (from a recent *TAP Air Portugal* press release — "*For information call 0207-434 7246*")

Sending staff abroad 3.17

Organizations which are not travel agencies tend to be not so good at arranging this kind of trip — and making the most suitable arrangements. So consider dedicating a member of staff to this — and to the whole process if you are sending staff abroad, setting up a new operation, or even relocating your business to another country.

This would be for travel and accommodation, and all aspects of the relocation, someone who has a knowledge of work and the business environment in that country, and knows what moving to another country is like

Staff transferred abroad 3.18

When you are working abroad, your contribution — and the risk you have taken — will often not be valued as much as if you had stayed at home. Like the army, one of the first rules of international working life can be 'Never volunteer!'

Which seems the wrong way of looking at it. Also, out of sight, sadly, is often out of mind in many organizations, when it comes to promotions and a longer-term career.

On the plus side, much of the planning and paperwork will be done for you — which puts you in a slightly different world from those independent working travellers who organize work abroad themselves.

Which will often be reflected in your physical circumstances: the international glass-and-steel hotels where international business people often are; while their more independently-minded colleagues are often in the grass hut on the beach past the shanty town somewhere down the road. I exaggerate, but not by much

Independent travel-and-work 3.19

Meaning you are not posted there by your company. You go there yourself.

It might be on your own, or with a friend, or travelling companions, or with a group of like-minded volunteers, when you go to travel and work abroad.

This means you can have very different goals from the business traveller; and very different expectations about buying plane tickets and arranging hotels — when you are doing all these things and paying for them yourself

After you arrive 3.20

And this difference between the two groups — 'independent' and 'company' travellers — the paid for and the paying — is one which will persist after you arrive, in the kind of people you meet, and socialize with; in where you live; and in a surprising number of other ways.

You can still spend some of your social life in the big hotels — if that is what you want —even when you are living in the grass hut by the beach — see above — but these are really two very different groups of international workers: those who go mainly because they have to; and those who may decide to get a job abroad themselves, and then perhaps get one on the spot.

There are shades of grey in between — where people volunteer through a large organization, and then get assigned a job abroad. Or a career which begins 'independently' in a foreign country; and then continues with a particular organization or company.

Remember to register with your embassy

Doing it your way 3.21

If you are arranging your trip to a new life, or summer work, or retirement, yourself, you also can do this in the way which suits you — by approaching an agency for work — like the ones which exist for au pairs or summer camps — or approaching other potential employers in an area of work you want to do — or seeing property agencies and agents — or going to look for a new home there, or just by going it alone and turning up.

Again, it depends on who you are But it is quite realistic — with just a little forward planning — to make any one of these arrangements for yourself

Earning money and moving around 3.22

Will you try to earn some money and pay for your trip before you go, or to continue your travels and earn some money 'on the way' — a high-risk but more adventurous strategy? If travelling the world is your priority, and seeing strange exotic places, you should not be too disappointed if you do not actually get to see so much of it, or travel around. That is what work is.

Even those who spend their time travelling and working — like airline pilots and hostesses — complain that they spend most of their time in hotel rooms, and never have time to see the countries they visit . . .

So if you are going through an agency to work — or travel — or volunteer — abroad, how much free time will you have? Have a realistic expectation of what is involved — and remember work carries some responsibilities too

Travelling alone 3.23

Some people like to; some people don't. Travelling alone — and going there and setting up home by yourself — can be the most difficult challenge of all; but sometimes the most rewarding; as there can be many compensations if everything goes well. There is an advantage in making local friends, or having made some plans for where to live, and a job — or if these have been made in advance by someone you know — for yourself.

And many difficulties. But there is a good side to this. When you are with a group — on some overland expedition-cum-adventure holiday to the 'heart' of Africa — it is this group which is at the centre of everything you do every day, for instance, and not any other people you might meet *en route*.

You are like a group of travelling expatriates, strangers in a strange land. The adventure is not quite what it seemed; and a stifling atmosphere can be created. This is one version of travel which, strangely enough, is becoming more popular, but is really more like an adventurous package tour.

But if you go somewhere to work on your own, to get a job, or just to live there for a while, or follow an interest you have, you are much more likely to meet local people than if you lived in some expatriate colony far away out of town — or even far away from anywhere in some weird hippy colony like 'The Beach;' or get caught up in some world where the way of life includes a fierce nostalgia for the place you thought you had left behind: English pubs, Irish bars . . . you can find these anywhere; and are places where you could find the English-speaking and international expatriates of your *locale* — anywhere.

But it is best — except in the circumstance which greets Leonardo DiCaprio in the movie to be 'off the beach' and away from the beaten track, and where the locals are

Travel, or work? 3.24

Which is most important for you, travel or work?

This is the big decision you will make. Which comes first, so far as *you* are concerned: earning money to travel, or travelling in order to work?

One will involve using your own resources — whether you are going it alone, or with companions; the other will involve working with people there — and you will be connected to the locality in a different way.

And working or volunteering abroad — or even a business transaction or study visit — all offer a much more 'authentic' way of encountering the country and its people, however you do it; or having any reason for being there which goes beyond just tourism. This could be bird-watching, butterfly collecting . . . whatever it may be . . . but any one of these would be a good reason to mix an interest you have with travel.

Or getting a job there. This applies to your work and life outside work too. If you can follow an interest like this you will find out what life there is really like; and escape an experience like that of being on a package holiday or guided tour — or being trapped on that jungle expedition with a group of gap-year students.

When you are travelling alone — or living abroad — you can use your own resourcefulness and skills to get the most out of your trip. And when you get there, having a hobby or interest helps

An interest 3.25

It is a good idea to maintain your hobbies and interests when you get there; and this is one thing you can take which is as important as any of the above if you will be living in a new country — which will bring some continuity to all these changes. .

It is what you bring yourself to each new experience which counts. However far you go, you will never leave yourself behind

Driving 3.26

Going by car is one option — one way would be to take it with you. But you may well find you are better off selling your old one, and maybe buying a car when you get there. Where to get your international driving licence is one question — usually from your local automobile association, like the *AA* in *Britain*, or *AAA* in the *USA*, which are now both on the internet — *www.theaa.co.uk* and *www.aaa.com*. Will this licence need a translation in the local language for instance?

The address of the local automobile club or association is something their embassy or tourist office could tell you, as well as sending you their travel and transport information; and all you would need to know about driving there. They can do this. Find out about the rules for exporting a car if it is more than 12 months old. And tell your insurers.

National tourist offices can often send their guides or magazines, or photocopied pages they produce themselves, about living and working in that country too.

One sent to me by the *German Tourist Office* (called *Germany: A Guide to Living and Working in Germany* — Rios Werbung GmbH, Eschersheimer Landstr. 69, 60322 Frankfurt/Main, *Germany*; tel +49-69 5 97 00 91; fax +49-69 5 96 22 27) has no less than five pages on driving, and traffic signs: "*Germans take their driving seriously; and Americans are often amazed by the speed at which they fly along the country's well maintained super highways . . . Motorists from non-European Union countries may drive for up to a year in Germany with a license from their homeland or an international driver's license. Not those from the EU . . .*"

There is more; about where to get a translation of this licence if you need one; regulations for children — that children under 12 are not allowed to ride in the front seat for instance — speed limits — 100kph (62 mph) even on some winding secondary roads — and what to do if you live in *Germany* and drive. "*Many Americans assume that passing in an intersection is prohibited, so they fail to properly watch for rear traffic at least twice and, because of the rear view mirror's 'blind spot', should not rely on it alone.*" And perhaps get crushed by German heavy goods vehicles.

This booklet also has sections including a 'Map of Germany', 'Where to Live', 'Residence Permits', 'Customs and Courtesies', 'Working in Germany', 'Banks and Banking', 'Embassies and Consulates', 'Voting', 'Mail Services', 'Taxes', 'Telephones', 'Adapting', 'Continental Airlines Report', 'Train Travel', 'Driving', 'Traffic Signs', 'International Schools', 'Moving and Relocation Services', and 'Facts at Your Fingertips' — a well-thought out guide

The Swiss tourist office sent a more standard brochure — *Welcome to the Best of Switzerland* — which seems to be subtitled 'Don't Miss the Swiss' — with a suitable colour map of regional and local roads, information on 'Getting to Switzerland', '. . . and around Switzerland', 'Classic Panorama Tours', 'Cities', 'Summits', and

'Switzerland Travel Tips' — and tourist driving requirements are in one section as well:

"... *Alpine passes are easy to drive, but reasonable care must be taken on more narrow, winding roads. Passes can be avoided where there are road tunnels or car trains. Speed limits are: freeways 120 km/h (75 mph); highways 80 km/h (50 mph); and cities / towns 50 km/h (31 mph), An annual road toll called the 'Vignette' is levied on all cars and motorcycles using the freeways. Cars rented in Switzerland usually include the Vignette; vehicles rented outside do not. Vignettes are available at border crossings as well as all Swiss post offices and gas stations.*"

This is the kind of thing you can easily get hold of. You can't always easily find these guides produced for foreign visitors when you are there, so contact the tourist information office — and they should be able to some brochures and leaflets — for driving and living there.

Statistically, driving is one of the most dangerous ways you can travel; local buses and aeroplanes are safer means of transport — with rail and then coach travel not far behind. Also find out about local driving conditions and parking regulations

By truck — removal companies 3.27

If you are heading further afield, or if transport is part of your job, then your own transport association (like the *Freight Transport Association* in the *UK*, Hermes House, St. John's Road, Tunbridge Wells, Kent; tel 01892-526171) is where to go first. Your household goods would go by road if the place is closer to home; by air if not — where you should consider how much you really need to take, or what can be sold in a garage or car-boot sale before departure, or passed on to luckless relatives.

In Britain, *the* British Association of Removers *can be your contact for removal companies: 3 Churchill Court, 58 Station Road, North Harrow HA2 7SA, UK; tel 0208-861 3331. Ask for their useful checklist of things to do before moving — and their leaflet for people who are moving abroad. And see* Direct Contacts

Off-road travel 3.28

If you have to set up an operation somewhere in the desert, or far from home, or if you are organizing an expedition to a remote spot, see the *Vehicle-dependent Expedition Guide* — with all the technical background on planning, equipment, people, vehicles and operations.

The 'Vehicle-dependent Expedition Guide' by Tom Sheppard, published by Desert Winds — *in association with* Land Rover — *44 Salusbury Lane, Hertfordshire SG5 3EG, UK; ISBN 0-9532324-0-9*

Maps 3.29

Maps — of almost anywhere — are in your local bookstore,or travel bookshop, or library. Also see under *Guides and Maps* in *Sources of Information*.

The tourist office can probably send some useful ones too

Beating jetlag 3.30

'Darkness holds the key for jet-lag sufferers,' says the headline. In an article in the *Journal of the Royal Society of Medicine*, researcher Jim Waterhouse says the secret is the time — about 5am usually

— when your 'core' body temperature drops to its lowest. "*Exposure to light after that point helps the body clock to advance; exposure to light before the core temperature minimum is reached helps to delay it.*"

If you are travelling west, and need to put your body clock back, you need lots of light between 9pm and 3am, before you are going. "*This fits in better with local daylight hours,*" Mr Waterhouse says (and so it seems human physiology is better designed for a journey from east to west). In the other direction, you could try preparing by getting up — and getting some exposure to light — early in the morning. "*But when you get there you will find you need to stay indoors all morning to reset your clock.*"

Flying from west to east, you can remain awake for the first part of your flight; and half-way through doze or sleep if you can. On arrival stay awake, until the time you would normally go to bed. And stay indoors until late in the mornings for the first few days

Stay up and sleep in. Also, people going on long flights, especially those with heart or circulation problems, should make a point of getting a little exercise and walking up and down the aisle at regular intervals

Basic medical supplies 3.31

Vitamins — general vitamins or vitamin C; Clove oil and sensitive toothpaste — for toothache; Paracetamol or similar; Insect repellant gel, cream, spray, mosquito nets . . . ; Lipsalve or balm; Some antiseptic cream; Plasters . . . and then perhaps suntan cream; And your medical records / vaccination certificates / allergy information; Contraceptives; Antibiotics for diarrhoea; Anything you personally need — or for your family — like asthma treatments, pills for travel sickness, stomach upsets; Something for sore throats and colds — like Lemsip. A visit to your local pharmacy, or even one in the airport, is a good idea.

The most common health problem abroad is diarrhoea; with the hotter countries where sanitation is a problem the chief culprits for this condition, which can vary in severity; and used to be called, in former times, 'Delhi belly' — but is unfortunately a problem in some countries in southern Europe as well. This is not necessarily due to the water, but because you meet a different population of the bacteria which, in any case, are in everyone's digestive system; and which you are not used to.

It comes from the food as much as water; but you should drink boiled or bottled water; and use this even when cleaning your teeth in these places; avoid unboiled milk; soft fruit; seafood; and ice-cream here — even ice in your drinks. Take with you water purification tablets — or similar gadgets — and a drug such as *Lomotil* or *Imodium.*

This is the advice of the Digestive Disorders Foundation, *PO Box 251, Edgeware, Middlesex HA8 6HG, UK. Send them a stamped addressed envelope — or equivalent* International Reply Coupons *— and see under this heading in* Living there, 5.29 *— for a leaflet*

YHA Adventure Shops *sell a range of adventure travel items. Head office: 19 High Street, Staines, Middlesex, TW18 4QY,* UK; *tel 01784-458625. Contact them for a catalogue. Or* "Read our essential guide for travel equipment and safety and browse through our range of products on *www.yhaadventure.co.uk.*" *These include medical kits, mosquito nets, and other useful devices*

Some other things to take 3.32

You can also buy a range of travel items at your local chemist's or supermarket, ranging from 'refresher' tissues — like the ones which airlines provide — to a travel element for boiling water, like a kettle — and some disposable-type plastic cups

Also take: some stamps; stationery; writing paper; a notebook or file; paperback books; a laptop computer (of the kind you can hook up to the internet); or mobile phone / reduced-rate phonecards; names and addresses of family and friends; a travel or 'world' radio — see 4.20 — and a small digital alarm clock; miniature hi-fi / CD player; some CDs / CD-ROMs / DVDs (these are light and travel well) CDDDVCDs (sorry, these haven't been invented yet!); a few pages photocopied from a travel guide — for example this list — and a photocopied piece of paper with all your practical details on — and see below. If you are going to a cold country, warm clothes; and if you are going to a warm one, cool ones.

If in doubt, dress up rather than down. In general, get some information about the country — and the climate — and then take the minimum. Wearing several layers of clothing, and having waterproof boots, is the way to be warm in a cold country . . .

Think of all the things you take on a weight to usefulness ratio. All the above pass this test

Pets 3.33

You are prohibited from taking parrots into *Poland*; There will be rules everywhere for the import of certain kinds of animals — and a changing *régime* in *Britain* which now means you can take your newly microchipped pet more easily in and out of the country.

You should contact the embassy of that country; and mainly your vet to find out what needs to be done beforehand. Is there such a thing as international pet insurance? Whether your pet passes the weight to usefulness test is up to you

A checklist of what needs to be done before your move 3.34

And also see the *Key Points* at the end of this chapter. This is:

to make a list of all items to be moved — and what to store or sell . . . and . . .

purchase some black binliners, or similar, and get hold of some suitable cardboard boxes

donate old clothes and unwanted items to charity, or have a 'garage' sale. See what you don't want or need, and store the rest

And involve the children — if you have some! — They should decide what they want to take themselves

get a leaflet from your local post office about mail — and see Chapter 5 for more about The post office and its services

and contact your bank, telephone company, electricity / gas company, landlord or estate agent, doctor, dentist, passport office, children's school, insurance company, employer, vet . . . all the 'official' people who need to be contacted. Have a session on this. This reads like a list of similar people who have to be contacted when you arrive too . . .

Make a note of important telephone numbers — personal and family ones — and useful ones when you get there, like the embassy — again — your bank, and insurance / credit card / building society; a photocopy of your passport and driving licence — and take details of any subscriptions or store cards you have . . .

And you should remember to:

obtain full insurance for everything being moved — and not move anything too valuable or difficult to move — your valuable china, or tropical fish, and tropical china or valuable fish

get hold of health records from the doctor, and your dentist's and optician's records

leave a forwarding address — perhaps a map — with family, friends, colleagues. A local map of how to get there will probably be needed by your removal company too

contact a removal / freight company well in advance, contacting two or three for a quote. Like OVERS — tel 0800-24 34 33; *or* Lowes of Chester — 01244-373286. *See Direct Contacts*

and double-check all the documentation you need with that country's embassy — also with any countries en route *if you are driving there — also check about imports / exports / currency*

label your boxes — packing the important things yourself

Not if you are heading off to a secret island of course, when you could try rafting there, if you can find a map . . .

Empty the loft, cupboards, garage, garden shed . . . (don't take plants or seeds out of the country unless you know the rules for importing them into your new one)

check your insurance cover again

have your car serviced if you're leaving this way

find out about the import-export rules

And make a start as soon as you can. Three months before is not a bad time to begin

Send some postcards,with your new address, to friends and family when you get there! Unlike DiCaprio . . .

Getting there by plane or train 3.35

For long-haul trips, it will probably be better by plane — or, in Europe, or in *Japan*, by high-speed train. High-speed services — the *TGV*, or *Thalys*, or *AVE* — or *Shinkansen* — and also the *Channel Tunnel* and *Eurostar* in *Britain*, *France* and *Belgium* — tel 0990-388388 and 0990-186186 — or at *www.eurotunnel.com* or *www.eurostar.com* — are very often a comfortable way of getting there in good time.

You are advised to avoid the high season, and to book your seat. Contact the national tourist information centre or your local travel agency for the right local contacts

By boat 3.36

Ferry and hovercraft companies operating to and from Britain:

Brittany Ferries: 0870-536 0360

Condor Ferries: 01305-761551

Hoverspeed: 0870-525 0241

P&O Stena Line: 0870-600 0600

SeaFrance: 0870-571 1711

Otherwise, ask your local travel agency about local ferry services to or from that island to the mainland . . . In many places there will be useful ferry services.

You can contact the local tourist office. Nationally, they may also publish a *Tour Operators' Manual* — a very important document for all kinds of contacts like these — for people arranging tourism to that country for instance, for tour operators — and for you.

Ferries and their details will be in here; but also many other useful contacts; facts and figures; names and addresses; hotels and restaurants — and everything from the local national holidays to shop opening times, the kind of information which professionals use, but you can too.

These can be the best guides of all, for visitors and anyone staying a longer time, intended for tour operators and travel agents but useful also for you

Liners and cargo boats 3.37

Another way out would be by liner or cargo boat — an unusual way to emigrate; but for many not so long ago it was quite a usual way to go, before air travel became easier.

Now, a trip on a cargo boat will more like taking a specialized cruise — but if you were off to somewhere like the Atlantic island of *St. Helena*, this might be still the only way: on the *RMS (Royal Mail Ship) St. Helena*, which stops off on its route to *South Africa* at St. Helena, *Ascension Island* and *Tenerife* — and once a year goes to the smaller island of *Tristan da Cunha*:

Curnow Shipping Ltd, *48-50 Killigrew Street, Falmouth, Cornwall TR11 3AP, UK; tel 01326-211466; fax 01326-212808*

By coach 3.38

Coaches go to many places. Ticket prices compare either very favourably or very unfavourably with charter flights. It depends.

If there was a fairly cheap air route it would usually be better to go this way, even paying a little extra, as you would not need so much time for the journey — a coach takes 24 hours or more from western to eastern Europe, or even from *Britain* to southern *Spain* — and you will not need so much money for the trip.

By coach, you would probably arrive closer to the city centre — which would be an advantage.

A long-haul journey like this is not everyone's cup of tea though. Indeed, there may not be a cup of tea at all. Take food, and wrap up warm in winter — but with a little preparation this can be a reasonable way to get there.

Check in an hour or two beforehand — like an airline — and check the luggage arrangements. and what you can take

Charter flights 3.39

European charter flights to the Mediterranean — *Spain, Italy, Portugal, Greece, Croatia, Turkey* . . . to all these places a flight will tend to be similar in price to a coach trip at many times of the year — making this a good way to keep up connections with home.

This is one reason, perhaps, why many people from northern Europe end up living in these Mediterranean places; and seasonal workers come from places like Italy to *Britain*, or Spain to *Holland* . . . outside the tourist season. Mind you, there may not be too many flights *out* of somewhere like *Menorca* in winter.

It is the same in the southern states of the *USA*, places like Miami or Las Vegas which have shown a similar growth of both seasonal workers and retirees; and there is also a movement of people north — for other economic reasons — from these holiday destinations of the south. Many people move south to retire, or change their way of life, from Waikiki to Western *Australia*, the Algarve to *Argentina*, and often go from the richer countries to the less rich ones — a pattern which is repeated everywhere.

Some times of the year are cheaper than others for charters: April / May . . . or September / October. Charter flights — and cheap air travel generally — really are making a difference to the choices people can make and the ambitions they have about where in the world they might live and work — and have brought the possibility a holiday home in Florida or a winter break in *Tunisia* much closer to many than it ever was before.

No longer is the idea of an expatriate lifestyle or a retirement in the sun a dream only of the very rich. Many more people nowadays are considering living — and working — or retiring — or doing business — abroad

Key Points

Consider local customs and sensibilities

Read the newspapers. Keep up with the political — and exchange rate — and air fares — situation

Find out more about visa requirements

Contact your own Foreign Office *or* Foreign Ministry

Shop around for tickets — and check two or three different sources of information — and see if all airport taxes are included

Also see other products you buy for any special offers

Book early — the price of air tickets tends to go up the closer the departure date gets — and airlines tend to price their tickets in four 'seasons' — so the exact date of departure can make a big difference to the price

Pay by credit card if you can — see if they have insurance which applies to travel

Make sure the agency is part of your national association for travel agents, and for air tickets part of IATA (International Air Transport Association, tel +41-22-7992525, fax +41-22-7983553, www.iata,org) — *or in the* UK *has the* ATOL Air Travel Organiser's Licence (ATOL) — *a legal requirement for agencies selling air tickets and protecting travellers from being stranded abroad*

If you pay a deposit your receipt should include flight number, airline, dates

Make a photocopy of legal / official documents, like your passport — and this receipt — and leave these with someone at home — and take copies with you — see Basic medical supplies <u>3.31</u> *and* A checklist of what needs to be done before your move <u>3.33</u> *previously*

This might include any allergies you have, medical certificates and documents you need, for example for vaccinations, your passport number and a contact at home, and for your embassy / hotel / residence; your travel insurance details and world-wide contact number to call in case you do need medical treatment — or money transfer — and take some spare passport photos . . .

You can sort out what you want to take — and leave behind. But you can do a lot when you get there too. Take the minimum!

Contact your national trade association for removals — and then contact some removal companies. Three months is a reasonable time to allow for an international move like this

And check in in good time

Questionnaire

Your name: *age:* *profession:*

Address: *tel:* *e-mail:*

Relevant qualifications and experience

What do you want to do?

Which country / destination do you wish to work in?

Would you be looking for work from home or on the spot?

Do you require immigration / visa and work permit information?

Would you like to receive contacts for organizations recruiting now?

Do you require any personal contacts for people / organizations there?

Please give details of other areas / jobs you are interested in

Would it be OK for you to be a contact for others moving there in future?

This page may be photocopied ***x 142 % / 1.42*** *to produce an A4 page*

Please feel free to attach any longer answers to these questions; we will send a background dossier for your destination, with the work, travel, visa details you request and / or other useful information, and a range of contacts for employment. The fee for this service is £48 / $80, payable to 'Speak English'

English Contacts Abroad, *PO Box 126, Oxford OX2 6UB, UK*

English Contacts Abroad is an information / research service, not a recruitment agency; it is important for you to check credentials of individuals / organizations mentioned yourself

4

Settling in

"When you are settling in, your own understanding of yourself and who you are is most important . . ."

And the motivation needed for any job — or any trip — must come from you, and not from any careers manual or guide book — even this one.

This chapter is about Settling in, *beginning with* Preparation *and ending with some* Key Points *to consider*

Preparation 4.1

You are recommended to do your research in advance and your preparation for yourself — and also not to take any single source of information for granted.

Stories of hapless backpackers straying into *North Korea* during their intended trip to *China* are true. 'Richard' in 'The Beach' strays into a field full of marijuana, surrounded by armed guards... It should never happen — and this applies to all the other pitfalls to do with this change in your way of life, which you should try to anticipate . . . Many problems — large and small — can be avoided if you do just a little checking and research in advance.

A good piece of advice — for your preparation — is never rely too much on just one source of information, guidebook or map. You will get a much more rounded picture from two or more different sources

Research 4.2

You may get help, if you end up in some desperate straits, from your local embassy or consulate. Or you might not. Make use of this source of information before you go, though; and contact them before you get there — not after something goes wrong.

You will get less sympathy if you have not taken all possible precautions not *to get into the trouble you find yourself in*

Knowing yourself 4.3

When it comes to settling in, your own understanding of yourself — and why you are going there in the first place — will be most important, and who you are. You could say this is the key to a successful future in any area of life — a saying known to philosophers down the ages: *Know thyself.*

Wherever you go, but especially if you move to a different country and strange surroundings, knowing the answer to these questions will be most important. And if you have your own personal objective, keep this in mind, and not to lose sight of your goals

One thing you can always find out more about when you travel is: yourself . . .

Learning from experience 4.4

Consider what you know now about the country; what you expect. Do not forget your preconceptions; but be ready to learn from experience. You could make a list of advantages and challenges here. What are the positive and negative points you associate with that place, with your trip or with your new job? . . .

It depends on your point of view. Your expectations, which you can expect to change, or be changed — in the weeks and months which lie ahead. So be flexible, and prepared to make changes, in the way you see the world. This will also help you settle in

On arrival 4.5

You would find it easier — even if this is for only a few days — leaving a little time at the beginning to make all your own practical arrangements, before you start work.

There may be some tax advantages, too, in taking some time to get there, or having a break between your departure and arrival. *See Chapter* 5, 5.18, 5.19

Hospitality 4.6

Generally, you should accept any invitations which come your way, and hospitality. Approach these in a positive frame of mind (but with caution if it is like the one which greets 'Richard' at the start of 'The Beach.' Some you can ignore . . .).

Often, moving into a new neighbourhood, getting to know your neighbours — or, at work, your colleagues — will take a long time.

This may be quicker in another country, as the slow process of getting to know your 'locality' of acquaintances / neighbours / colleagues tends to accelerate, especially in the first few days / weeks when you get there.

Moving to a new country speeds up this process of getting to know people, in your street or in your workplace. On the other hand, it can be difficult to get to know people well. You may find you do this more easily at the beginning — so now is the time to make contacts and meet some of the friends you will know during the rest of your stay.

What are your ideas about other people? And who you are? These are the key. In fact, they are everybody's starting point for meeting people and embarking on a new stage of life

Corona Worldwide 4.7

Corona Worldwide also offers a briefing service for people going abroad, where you can meet someone who has been to that country or speak to them over the telephone. For more on the different kinds of briefing they offer, see 5.24 and 5.25.

Corona Worldwide, c/o The Commonwealth Institute, Kensington High Street, London W8 6NQ, UK; tel / fax 020-7610-4407; e-mail hq@coronaww.prestel.co.uk; *www.commercepark.co.uk/coronaww/*

This is one way to find out more from people who have already been there

Practical contacts 4.8

You should have some more practical contacts as well; and prepare these: a telephone number for a nearby GP, or dentist, or local pharmacy . . . list of estate agents, a garage; or look at the driving regulations, a map of the area, and so on — and do some background research.

How? The embassy on the spot will have contacts / names and addresses for local expatriate organizations, and the people who run them; and your local — or rather the 'international' — community there, who have their own activities and meeting places.

This would be a good practical contact, a very important one. So call or contact the embassy.

You could get in touch with these international or expatriate organizations this way; or find a list of property agents; or find out about local clubs and societies which may exist — and all kinds of useful things about trade and commerce as well, business and getting a job there, buying a house, finding a property agency ...

And often, a local English-language or expatriate publication exists — and is a good thing to get hold of before you arrive. This really can help you get to know the place even before you get there.

This is where the names and addresses can be found for many practical needs, for everything from bookshops to veterinary practices — and the many commercial organizations who want to be in touch with you — and the local international community — just as in a local newspaper back home.

These international magazines, pocket guides and newspapers also have this advantage over any guidebook, that they will be more up to date. *See* 4.9, 4.10, 4.11, 4.12

An international newspaper 4.9

One such would be for the Hungarian capital Budapest — where quite a large American and English-speaking community is to be found. *The Budapest Sun*, 1122 Budapest, Városmajor utca 13, *Hungary*; tel (361) 214-0390; fax (361) 214-0388; e-mail letters. editor@bpsun.hu or info@bpsun.hu) contains restaurant reviews, events, articles on people and places, a 'community calendar' of clubs and societies, and their meetings of interest to expatriates, and classified ads for everything from apartments to washing-machines, to international schools; some useful and interesting feature articles; listings for English-language church services; TV programmes and films also in English; and a 'Style' and 'Home' supplement; as well as local, international and business events.

And a thousand and one other things, in a slightly Hungarian style ("*Having slumbered since New Year, Old Man Winter is up and taking it out on us*")

Local city guides 4.10

Local city guides, or 'What's On' guides exist almost everywhere. Again they have this advantage, that they are locally produced and are up-to-date; and may be brought much closer to anyone possessing this method of communication by the Internet and the World Wide Web — although you can still contact them yourself, direct. They are not just on-line; but somewhere out there in the non-virtual world too.

For even the non-English-speaking countries, there will be these guides, mainly in English, which have spread almost everywhere — another development which happened during the 1990s which will help expatriates and people thinking of living and working abroad today. All of which is changing the face of guide books and travel.

These city guides tend to be produced by some kind of collaboration between expats and the locals

Vilnius in Your Pocket 4.11

Opening a copy of *Vilnius In Your Pocket*, the "*official guide*" to the Lithuanian capital (PO Box 52, 2000 Vilnius-C, *Lithuania*; tel +370 2-22 29 76/61 20 40; fax +370 2-22 29 82; e-mail: viyp@post.omnitelnet; *www.inyourpocket.com)*, I find the following e-mail has been included in this edition:

"*I'm sick and tired of relying on guide books that rely on travelers writing in to amend, whilst you lot sit and do nothing except take barrowloads of money to the bank every day*" — a sentiment I would go along with (although the conclusion about money may not be quite right).

Still, guide books often rely on their student travellers / travelers to go around, and send in reports; and are often second-hand or impressionistic. Which will not be as interesting for longer-term visitors as this sort of publication, produced by local people.

You could get hold of this pocket guide to the Lithuanian capital yourself — by contacting your Lithuanian Embassy, or writing to the Lithuanian Tourist Office . . . and the same applies for other places, almost everywhere. The contents list includes *Bookshops, Getting There, Basic Data on Lithuania, Lithuania Through the Ages, The Road to Independence, Where to Stay, Where to Go Out, Vilnius By Night, Entertainment, Street Register, Maps, What*

To See, Jewish Vilnius, Out of Town, Trakai, What to Buy, Communications, Trolley Bus Scheme, Useful Addresses, Officials, Media, A People and Their Trees, Sports and *How Well Do You Know Vilnius?*

And even the ads would be useful for a first-time visitor, especially for anyone going to live or do business there. On the facing page we find that "*DFDS Baltic Line offers you a four-weekly cargo service between Klaipeda and Denmark.*" Something you might need to know. Then there are the local travel agencies, hotels, or an international school, the bank for *Western Union Money Transfer*, and so on, all up to date, as this is produced by people who really know the place — because they live there.

This is a representative example of any city guide around the world — which can beat any 'Lonely Planet' or 'Rough Guide' book hands down for what you want to do. And if you are wondering what 'Trakai' is, read on . . .

In a Lithuanian forest . . . 4.12

This kind of publication tends to contain the odd spelling mistake, it's true, but where else would you find advice like: "*Ticks — found a tick? No need to get paranoid. We here have decided to debunk the myths and give you the straight facts on ticks, and lyme disease . . .*" ? I won't worry you with the details — of interest all the same if you off to some northern forest — but suffice it to say that not all of these little animals are infected, and you should tuck in trousers and cuffs to try to deter them — "*in other words, dress like a nerd.*"

Which is what people recommend for mosquitoes, in fact. And, when you find one, "*try Vaseline, a hot match and tweezers to delicately pry out the little blood-sucker. The object of the game is to get the whole tick off and into a glass jar for testing."*

A list of symptoms follows.

That's enough about ticks, but you get the idea; and should you ever find yourself in this situation, you would know what to do if and when you find yourself in a Lithuanian forest — and what not to wear in *Lithuania*.

This kind of first-hand account will also give you greater insight into how the locals see themselves — and what to do and where to go

A list of opportunities 4.13

What are the opportunities? Here are some general ones which you can look at in the light of your own experience — but these will include:

Meeting people from your own and other countries, as well as the locals

A social life that will certainly be different

A new landscape, a new climate

New ways of looking at things, new discoveries to be made

Learning a new language

The enjoyment of meeting a challenge, and succeeding

You could add to this list those things which you think are important about the opportunities your trip will bring

Learning languages 4.14

The differences between them are not so great. In fact, their main rules — or 'deep structure' — are basically the same; as is the physical orgin of language as air from the lungs, which we shape with the vocal cords, and the other organs of speech: These are the mouth, the lips, the nose, the teeth, hard and soft palates, and the tongue.

This is all language is, in a physical sense. The author Anthony Burgess told me this when I interviewed him, some time ago now, about his book *A Mouthful of Air — language and languages, especially English* (Hutchison). This is a good one to consult, for all language learners — and their teachers — to give the reader a grounding in what learning a language is all about.

Which doesn't mean just watching foreign-language TV programmes. It doesn't work — I wish it did! Otherwise millions of Britons would now have a basic knowledge of Spanish. Just watching and listening are not enough — although you can learn something by seeing how speakers of other languages make the sounds they make.

You have to *do* something. Which probably means taking some lessons, individually, or in a school; or on a 'language holiday' abroad. Or getting hold of a book-and-cassette course.

Il Sillabo — a language school in Italy, not far from Siena and Florence in Tuscany — offers language and culture courses. "*It is easier to make friends — and accommodation is better priced than in other towns crowded with tourists,*" they say.

"*Our school is a small, family-run one, with a maximum number of 50 per month. The* Cultural and Social Program *includes visits to the main cities in Tuscany, like Siena, Pisa, Arezzo . . . walking through Florence and its famous sights . . . the wine . . . the food ... films . . . and our professional teaching methods are based on communication."*

Il Sillabo, *Via Alberti, 31, San Giovanni Valdarno (AR), Tuscany, Italy, e-mail sillabo@tin.it,* www.sillabo.com, *tel+39-055-9123238, fax+39-055-942439*

And there are computer courses now which supposedly 'correct' your pronunciation . . . Firms which post staff abroad to a country where another language is spoken, and spend no time or make no effort preparing their staff for this, or helping them to learn the language, are just not serious about this.

In fact, the foreign language you study will have much in common with your own. And some study which would include this — about all languages and how they work — would be useful in schools too; and for people learning later in life. A pity — in *Britain* — that it doesn't happen.

"*You see, there are thousands of languages in the world . . . You can't learn them all. How many can you manage to learn in a lifetime, you know, with moderate proficiency? Two or three at the outside, three or four,*" Anthony Burgess told me.

"*But don't teach languages, teach the whole principle of language, and say: 'Right, now you're going to Oslo next month, or you go to Oslo in six weeks, you'd better start learning Norwegian, enough to get around.'*"

For more about Anthony Burgess's life as an English teacher abroad see the forthcoming Straightforward *guide to the subject; and his autobiography 'Big Wilson and Little God.' And see under* Language courses 5.32 *in* Living abroad *for a useful cassette course; and under* TV *in this chapter, for more about the* Open University . . .

Health 4.15

The *E111* applies to all EU citizens — and some other European countries too — and is the document you need for just short-term travel in one of these, if you are travelling in Europe. In the *UK*, there is a useful booklet, *Health advice for travellers, anywhere in the world*, which comes with the application form; and has advice of use for almost anyone, anywhere; it would be useful to try and find one. Most easily, if you are there, this is at your post office.

Or it can be ordered by calling the *Health Literature Hotline*, tel 0800-555777. Or for more than 10 copies by writing to the: *Department of Health*, PO Box 410, Wetherby, Yorkshire, LS23 7LN.

Anyone from any of the European Union countries (and the European Economic Area, also Iceland, Liechtenstein *and* Norway) *is entitled to free or reduced cost medical emergency treatment in all the EU / EEA countries. You just need to fill in an application form and then to receive the E111 form itself, which is your 'passport' for emergency medical treatment in these places*

Also see under Healthcare *in* Living abroad — 5.35

Reciprocal healthcare agreements 4.16

These may be with any country. Your own foreign ministry or department of health — or physician or GP — can provide you with the details. An agreement like this — if there is one — entitles you to emergency treatment in that country — and for its citizens in your own. For example, a UK citizen can receive treatment in hospital free in *Australia* — and should *"make advance arrangements in the case of renal dialysis"* — but would pay charges for treatment at most doctors' surgeries, for prescribed medicines, ambulance travel and dental treatment.

In *Hungary*, treatment in hospital or at a doctors' surgery is free, for those coming from most other European countries; and you would pay for dental treatment or prescribed medicines yourself. In *Russia*, coming from any of the EU countries, you would receive free treatment in state hospitals, and pay for prescribed medicines. Also, in the EU, it will depend on whether your social security payments are up to date, and sufficient — and on the rules for local people and their health service.

All over the world, accident and emergency departments of public hospitals — and emergency dentists — are quite used to treating down-on-their-luck foreigners, as they would the locals, often for free. You are much more likely than not to find these, anywhere, offering the best service they can

Do you have to pay? 4.17

Only occasionally will you be asked for a payment for this kind of emergency — although this is is not true for all countries, like the *United States*. But this is a chance you probably can't take with your and your family's health.

So if the locals usually get private medical insurance, then it is better to do it this way. In many cases, an employer will include a private health scheme in the job package; but many self-employed people will have to do it themselves and should consider taking out a suitable but flexible insurance policy — for which they would have to pay.

Wherever you come from, contact the embassy or consulate of the country concerned, to find out what health care you would be entitled to if you move there

With health insurance it is better safe than sorry

Some insurance companies 4.18

Medicare International, *2 Minster Court, Mincing Lane, London EC3R 7FT, UK; tel 0207-816 2033; fax 0207-816 2123*

MediCover *(0870-735 3600 — The Courtyard, 16 West Street, Farnham, Surrey GU9 7DR, UK; fax 01252-717788). "Travellers with a medical condition could soon find it hard to arrange holiday insurance on standard terms,"* they say. *"Premiums are firming up and some insurance providers are being much tougher on travellers who have a medical problem."*

"T ypically, someone with a heart condition might now be expected to pay for the first £5,000—£10,000 of a claim. Or, cover may be limited to only £10,000 — a seriously inadequate sum if he requires emergency surgery in the US, *where treatment could cost £30,000 or as much as £50,000 for a triple- by-pass operation"*

MRL Insurance *(01737-552100) says it has has broadened its special worldwide, year-round, multi-trip travel insurance policy — which covers individuals and families for both business and holidays — to include trips of up to 60 days' duration — and for*

'Backpackers on extended stays' their current rate is £89 for four months worldwide, rising to £179 for a year

Also, ask if there is a national association of insurers you can contact — like the British Association of Insurers. *There will be one where you are, and one in the country you are moving to, which can tell you about local companies for your home or car insurance for instance*

Keeping fit 4.19

Sometimes, with all the socializing that is a part of moving to a new country — and often the drinking, which is a notorious part of 'expat' life from Alicante to Amazonia — you will really need to make an effort to do this, and keeping fit.

It will help later on, when some of the excitement begins to wear off maybe — a natural stage in this process of adapting to a new way of life.

You can easily begin to feel run-down or listless; which is also one effect of long journeys, or of being in a new country, the stress of starting,a new job — and a part of the process of acclimatization which happens to everyone.

Basic medical supplies will also be in your list of things to take — see Getting there 3.31

A world radio 4.20

A 'world' radio — one which picks up shortwave frequencies — is a good thing to have with you, especially in more remote places of the world where the dubious virtues of satellite TV have not yet left their imprint. A flick through the frequencies will show what is on offer, in terms of languages and programmes, broadcast on airwaves and satellite channels around the world. (Who, living or travelling anywhere in the world, has *not* done this on arrival, on some unknown shore?).

There may be some programmes in your language on FM or medium wave / AM which you can find; and the local easy-listening and rock and pop stations which are almost everywhere too

Also see Getting there *for more things you can take, which will help you adapt when you arrive* — 3.32

TV 4.21

The *BBC* now also has a worldwide television and 24-hour news service; and there are many other TV stations like *Sky* and *CNN* broadcasting around the world in languages from Russian to Ruthenian, well not quite.

To contact the BBC, or ask about subscribing to their worldwide programme guide 'On Air', write to: BBC World Service, *Bush House, Strand, London WC2B 4PH, UK; tel 0207-240 3456; fax 0207-257 8258; e-mail worldservice.letters@bbc.co.uk; http://* www.bbcnc.org.uk

To "*find out more about the* BBC Learning Zone *and what's on, visit our interactive and highly entertaining web site on* www.bbc.co.uk/education/lzone." *These* BBC Learning Zone *programmes also include some ones for the* Open University, *another worldwide institution — see* Direct Contacts, *and* 1.16, *Open University. Also see* 5.30, Language Courses, *and* www.Open2.net

Money 4.22

A stable financial situation — not necessarily a large income — will be vital — from the point of view of minimizing stress as well as in more obvious practical ways. For your own peace of mind, you need enough money — always — to be able to get home if you need to.

Companies who have experience of sending staff abroad include in their package elements like a free return air ticket and return visits home — especially important for destinations further afield; and health insurance, accommodation, and a living allowance

Some basic needs — organizations 4.23

If you are sending staff abroad, you should realize, as well as the basics — of where to live, food and accommodation, and all the necessary things of life — that there will be other requirements, which are not always visible ones, to help people settle in — especially where moving with a family is involved: the need for security being one; even to be valued for who you are; and within your organization or group — these are needs which anyone has, at home or abroad.

These are important, if hard-to-define. In another country, there may be a concern about safety for instance — which will not be so great if there are support systems around. People need this feeling of security on this 'secondary' as well as 'primary level,' of being valued for who they are, as well as having the basic necessities of life.

These are all called into question when moving to another country

Some basic needs — individuals 4.24

From your point of view, it will improve this process of settling in when there are these sources of security around — in the areas, of health, accommodation, money — so find out if there are any which your organization provides. . . and if there is a living allowance for expatriate staff for instance.

The value of the work you do will be correspondingly greater if there is someone who can provide support for staff posted abroad — and these primary and secondary needs are catered for. So food is important, personal safety . . . but so is self-esteem and being valued. Companies should see this kind of overall package as an investment in success — not an optional extra.

Think how complex it all is, this chain of tens, hundreds of events leading to your living and working abroad, or setting up a work or business project successfully in another country

There should always be someone in your organization you can go to at any of these stages

The five stages of living and working abroad 4.25

These are the five stages covered in this book — which individuals and organizations can and should consider too:

1. *Working abroad / life in the workplace*

2. *Getting — or being given — a job*

3. *Getting there, and travel arrangements*

4. Settling in

5. Living abroad / life outside work

Advantages of living and working abroad 4.26

These are not at all the same as the advantages of travel. "*On a personal level, there's the satisfaction of making a positive contribution to a developing economy.*" (This is what the charity VSO says about volunteering abroad). "*You'll be living and working for up to two years as part of a community with its own distinctive culture . . . so you'll be sharing skills . . . and building lifelong friendships.*"

"*But just as important is the chance to learn new skills and uncover hidden talents that will boost your career when you return.*"

Also, there are the experiences you will have — which sometimes you will look back on. Once I met a French engineer, who told me some stories that left a strong impression.

He worked in *Brazil* — on a dam — and he told me about returning home to find his wife, one day, in the rudimentary accommodation they had, running out of the kitchen, shouting something about a spider. The engineer went in to capture it — or so he thought — or frighten it away, before he too emerged, screaming, with a look of wild terror in his eyes.

"*It was this big, but this isn't what was frightening me. You see, when I went in there, it looked at me and jumped.*"

Aggressive, fearless, jumping spiders are certainly a disadvantage. There *are* some advantages to consider too:

Sometimes a cheaper way of life / cost of living

Cheaper property / accommodation

The chance to save

Job opportunities which you might not have at home

An international perpective on work and business

Sometimes a better climate

In a one survey of emigrants from Britain, *the weather was third on the list of reasons they gave for leaving the land of Shakespeare, with a better lifestyle and 'disillusionment' occupying the first and the second places. Surprisingly, 'better work opportunities' was only fourth, with 8% of those surveyed citing this as a reason for going*

And problems 4.27

To this list of advantages might be added some problems:

Meeting unexpected situations and events

Communications and transport

Accommodation

Social life and meeting people

The language

Practical questions like letters and bills — and bureaucracy

The health service and hospitals

Different ways of doing things

Missing family and friends — and keeping in touch

In all these areas international workers, and their families, will need sources of support and back-up from companies which send them abroad.

And be ready for some of these difficulties too, if you are travelling independently and making your own way

(Trakai 4.28

So, here we are. In case you were wondering, *Trakai* is a town surrounded by vast lakes and with a fairy-tale castle built by Grand Duke Gediminas some 25 km or so from Vilnius, also home to the Karaites, a Turkic ethnic group practising a religion akin to Judaism and counting under 200 members, with a national park information bureau, useful bookstore and city bus routes, petrol station, hotels, pensions, and sport base — "*No hot water, no drinking water and not much else either. Recommended only for the destitute or daring*"

— and a Yacht Club with "*two small rooms which they rent out;*" and places to go for picnics, seafood, beer, or the traditional Karaite *troškinta mėsa* stew or *kibinai* — "*like a British Cornish pasty*" — both served with a yeasty non-alcoholic drink, known as *gira*.)

Key Points

A secure foundation in the areas of health, accommodation and your living expenses will be important. But you will have to find a way to express yourself, and also find this sense of security in relation to other people, your colleagues and people you meet

5

Living abroad

"When you live abroad, anything can happen . . . You should prepare for the worst and enjoy the best of your stay"

The aim is *not* to end up like 'Richard' in 'The Beach' . . . You want to end up doing something worthwhile *off* the beach, not on it. But there is more to life than just work. This chapter is about living abroad: some practical things you can do to make your new life a success.

And see the Personal Experiences *in Appendix 3 for some real-life people who have done all kinds of jobs around the world*

Challenges and changes 5.1

When you live abroad, there will be challenges and changes: new neighbours, bills to pay, confusion about ever getting anything done… And when you are looking for somewhere to live, what even does a property agency look like? And what to do, how to get around if you don't speak the language?

How are you going to do any of these things — especially if you only know the country as a tourist? Living and working abroad is about a much closer contact with the country. You are not just going to get to know this new place on the larger scale of a guided tour or travelling around — so that if you came to *Britain* you might go interrailing to Inverness, or wherever. You are now going to get a 'close-up' of the country, of its people; and mainly staying in one place. The place you will know well is where you live — and work — and you are probably not going to travel about so much.

Which is obvious enough. Problems are different; but then so are the opportunities. One is language . . . and this is a time during which you could master many aspects which you would never be able to learn 'from a distance,' the pronunciation, phonology, everyday expressions and idioms . . . You will at least get to know some aspects of it better — by using it — and see 4.14.

Which applies to a lot of things — your relations with other people for instance — which, in or outside the workplace, is where the success or otherwise of your venture will really be measured. When you are dealing with people about many practical matters, they will be able to help you — if you can make yourself understood. But there is much more than merely this how-you-do-it side to living and working abroad. (Which is why this guidebook deals with more than just 'practical' matters).

One question this all raises is how well you get on with other people, for instance, *how* you get on with them . . . friends, or people that you meet; and one thing you find out will be your strong and weak points here.

This happens in many different ways, according to your situation — and I think mainly depending on your character; who you are — and think you are — your image of yourself and others; and your way of meeting and getting on with people — as some seem to make this transition to another country seamlessly, and without effort; and others take longer — but may get to know more about themselves, this new place, and this new stage in their lives too.

And one way to look at it is as series of stages — as Shakespeare did in his famous 'Seven Ages of Man' speech — which you move through and learn from. Wiser times and cultures have always seen life like this — and a good book about this theme is 'The Ages of Man' by J.A. Burrow (Clarendon Press, ISBN: 0198117558). It shows how this subject has been looked at down the ages.

Different ways of living might suit different times of life — and not just different places. That dilapidated doss-house in downtown Amsterdam may not suit someone who is older, and perhaps wiser. Cash may play a different role when you are older, too, and maybe we all end up muttering platitudes like Polonius . . . It depends how you look at it . . . and there are always compensations, however difficult the situation you find yourself in.

Again, you can think of all of these things as a problem — or an opportunity. Whichever way, you are not — if ever you were — in a dream world — DiCaprio again, and other anti-heroes of fiction — but this is your new reality, maybe harsh, or maybe hard to beat. And there is no reason to think you cannot succeed.

These are some of the basic questions which affect anyone going to live and work abroad. It's all a risk of course. A challenge. As life itself is

And in one sense, it doesn't matter much where you are from, and where you are going ... Without realizing this you could, if anything, make your life more difficult when moving to another country

Where to begin? 5.2

It begins with who you are. The first thing to know when you are living abroad, is that you will have to find new ways of doing things, and to think about your own aims and aspirations.

And you will discover different ways of life from when you were at home. How these differences strike you is one thing you will discover when you get there.

The art of living and working abroad is being aware of these circumstances, and knowing when to take the right risks — if you are looking for a job for instance, or during all these stages we have mentioned — and to avoid the dangers

And it must be in the context of what you *want to do; and being able to make the right decisions*

Three rules for living and working abroad 5.3

The first rule of living and working abroad — and looking for work — is never to entrust such an important decision to people who only say they have your best interests at heart; and are only intermediaries, middlemen — and some agencies. Many — for everything from moving to doing business to recruiting — will be reliable. Others will not.

The second is: you should answer questions like where you go, or what you want to do, yourself; and think about your own reasons for going and what you want to achieve.

The third is really a reminder: to contact local people, local organizations, local sources of jobs, as much as possible. You will be the person living and working there, after all; and you should take responsibility for each stage of your trip, each new step

Where to go 5.4

You really can go, almost anywhere around the world. Property agencies and magazines can be one starting-point — see the *Sources of Information* in Appendix 2 — and 5.37. And if you are thinking of getting away from it all, and *Malta* seems like a good place, or *Greece* — and maybe you have been there before — or you have studied Spanish — and Latin America seems a good option — or if you like the outdoor life and *New Zealand* seems the place to be — these are certainly all good options, and good reasons to be going. But you would need to find out more about the country and its people.

So contact their cultural centres, or embassies, tourist offices

A hobby or an interest 5.5

There are some ideas for where to go to find out more about living abroad at the end of this chapter — and in Appendices 1, 2 and 3 about *Direct Contacts, Sources of Information* and *Personal Experiences* . . . You really can get some ideas from what other people have done before. But the key point — if you have an interest in this country and some aspect of its way of life or culture — the food, the landscape, the places, the people, the language, the way of life . . . is first of all to have an interest; and then to *maintain this interest or hobby when you get there*

No firm plans? 5.6

Where can you start when you are thinking of moving abroad — and have no firm plans?

Learning more about the local history and culture — and the language — is one point of departure — and contacting your local college or university, where there might be courses you can do

Good and bad points 5.7

The interests you have can be one good reason for going, and can continue after you get there — and hopefully help get you through these changes, to adapt to living in this new country.

Which would apply to meeting and socializing with people, too, and your work environment; and all aspects of living there. Your job, your interests outside work, and your family, can each provide these elements of continuity between where you are now — and where you are going. You need something like this.

Also, if you have not already made a decision about your career, and it is this which is leading you to live and work abroad, you would have to think about this first of all, your work first, your interests second. Some clear thinking is needed.

For some, the job comes first. For others it might be the country, travel, study . . . or the main reason you have for going. Whatever it is, the motivation must come from you. This is how you are going to make sense of all the setbacks, as well as the opportunities you meet, what you anticipated and what you didn't expect . . .

There are all these unexpected problems which can make it difficult sometimes for expatriates 'overseas,' posted somewhere they didn't want to go, by a company or organization which does not seem to appreciate their efforts . . .

But life is like that, made up of all the things you didn't expect

Anything can happen . . . 5.8

Some people will prepare methodically; and move somewhere else after long thought, weighing up all the pros and cons, one by one. Some will make a more spontaneous decision — one which has been waiting, unseen and unexpected, for years; until suddenly they just up sticks and go. Going to live and work abroad can be like this too, and for an unexpected reason, something you didn't know was going to happen.

In either case, the idea that it is going to be you — and your family — who will have to take responsibilty for this decision is most important — even if you are the kind of person who prefers to go with the flow and take a more relaxed view of life

A kidnapping 5.9

And if you end up being kidnapped by a group of local guerillas when you are working in some dangerous part of the world — if this is a possibility — be sure that the sacrifice you are making has been worth it. Your employer will be still safe at home — and maybe willing to pay the ransom . . . But also, if you end up English teaching in some provincial city, travelling to and fro, from lessons in company after company, wondering why you are there, this is the time to consider coming home.

A great effort and a great change in your life is involved. You will have to know it has all been worthwhile. And there is more to life than just work . . .

A sense of adventure 5.10

Living in strange, exotic places, meeting exotic people, and exotic colleagues — all this can be part of the challenge; and the job satisfaction you can get from working as an engineer in Amazonia,, or doing business in *Uzbekistan*, will never quite be equalled by anything you could do anywhere else.

This is also how it can be. And the adventure can be part of the appeal of this kind of lifestyle, one which far outweighs the hazards. You will need to be cautious, and to make your preparations, but also a sense of adventure too

A secure foundation 5.11

It involves arranging your move successfully organizing accommodation for when you get there, and sorting out tax and financial matters, even for something as simple as making sure you have enough money to get by.

And making sure this new life — or period of your life — which you are making for yourself has a sure foundation

Permanent and non-permanent residency 5.12

Also see *Regulations for work permits – USA* in *Working abroad*

***Permanent resident** — all income is taxable, from the date you start work and become a resident.*

***Non-permanent resident** — only income from home which arrives in your new country is taxable, and what you earn there*

Where you are no longer a resident — in your old country, after you have left it — or anywhere you might go if you have left your old country and become a resident of somewhere else — you are just a visitor: for tourism, business, or study. But you still may return home to live, certainly while you remain a citizen of that country.

Even if you were born there, you are now officially a resident of the new one, though, for tax purposes; and you will have to make some arrangement for this — and if you want to keep your right to vote, for instance, when you are an expatriate living abroad

What is a resident? 5.13

You, now, are almost certainly a resident — and probably a citizen — in the place where you are. Certainly you live there — but this is not always the same thing as being a resident in the official sense of the word, which concerns the tax or social security authorities for instance.

If you go to another country for a period of over three or six months you will probably need a special visa or residence permit — and often a work permit of some kind. Perhaps an education visa for a year or two, for the period of your studies.

If you intend to go for any longer than any one tax year you will almost certainly be classed as a **resident** for tax purposes — even if you don't have some of the social security advantages of permanent residency — this happens if you are 'ordinarily living there,' the regulations say. And tax is basically difficult to avoid — see the tale involving the *Rolling Stones* below.

If you are intending to move now — or perhaps you have got a job already — you would be better off getting a residence permit straight away if you can — or as soon as you arrive, within the next day or two; and reporting to the local town hall / police station / immigration office where the relevant permits are issued

Better to do this. And your embassy or consulate there can tell you about these matters — or their embassy where you are. Letters of recommendation, and having all the right documents, are useful and necessary for immigration of any sort. You should make an inquiry about these: and contact the embassy first of all, not a visa agency

What you need 5.14

In most countries, you need this letter or offical form, completed by an employer, for a work permit, as well as evidence of where you live, to get a residence visa. Take some passport photographs for the application form / identity card — useful things to have.

If you arrive on a tourist visa, or don't have any of these other visas / permits, you can stay there as a tourist for a period of time; but you cannot work or become a resident there before you have contacted the relevant office on the spot and received permission for this or for work

What to bring 5.15

See *Getting there* (3.30, 3.31) for some useful items to bring — including your passport / visa — and evidence of where you used to live — of your previous employer and employment — as well as this letter of recommendation or immigration form from your current one.

You may need some documents like this to open a bank account; or install a telephone / electricity / household gas and so on; or for your new landlord; or to make a property transaction.

Tax years and tax bands 5.16

The point about tax is it works in years, tax — or 'fiscal' — years. This is the way allowances and tax benefits are calculated — everywhere. And almost everywhere you might reasonably expect to be has tax bands — a 'progressive' taxation system — 10%, 20%, 30%, or whatever — going up depending on how much you earn or have in income. There can be deductions for social security / national insurance or for health as well as a national income tax — and the local or state taxes may be correspondingly high.

In countries where the apparent income tax is low — like the *United States* — look out for high local or state taxes. You should find out what these are — like Council Tax in *Britain* — and if they apply to you — or if you should apply for a rebate.

There is a basic difference between countries where there is a relatively high personal allowance, up to which you don't pay any tax at all — or can get it back — and somewhere where a relatively low tax band starts quite early

Value Added Tax 5.17

The tax you pay in Value Added Tax or purchase tax will also affect the cost of living — again all information which can be supplied by the embassy / tourist office / *Ministry of Finance / Customs and Excise.*

When to leave 5.18

The country where you are a resident will be interested in your worldwide income, even if this has been taxed before in another country — unless there is a 'Double taxation agreement' — see below. But, very importantly, if you leave your country in the middle of the tax year — which might be from December 31 to January 1 or whenever this is — April 6 to April 5 as it is in *Britain*, then you can take advantage of the tax allowance for this period in both countries, which may be up to fifteen months.

This should be taken into account when considering your date of departure. There is more about tax and work in the Working abroad *chapter*

When to arrive 5.19

There can also be a gap between these dates — the day you leave the country and the day you start work — which it can sometimes be good to plan for, from this tax point of view — allowing time for travelling around in between.

This might be one way to see the world before you take up your new post in Belgium *or* Bali *— a long-drawn out move to a new country which, in some circumstances, your tax situation would favour*

Leaving your old tax system 5.20

Again this applies to going to your new country; or leaving for another one — or going home after you have become a resident of somewhere else. It is not easy to leave your old tax system behind.

Only when that tax year is finished, can you do this — and leave your old country for good, taxwise.

And you should still notify them — your current tax authorities, like the IRS in *America* or the Inland Revenue in *Britain* — straight away if you are becoming a resident of a new one. A point which is worth reemphasizing. Your tax form or declaration will probably be for part of that final year, which you would have to complete before you go, or even send home after you get there.

There would very probably be a tax declaration you would have to make in the new country too, even within 48 or 72 hours of arrival if you are going there to work, So two important addresses are your old and new tax offices

Joining a new tax system 5.21

If you are going abroad longer than a year, this change in your status — at home — will come into effect at the end of that tax year and the beginning of the next one, the following April 6 or January 1 — whenever the new tax year begins. Or after you have been mainly living there for a certain period of time. Your owning property there may also come into this.

You don't have to stay in the new country all the time, though,;even if you want to become a resident. This is where you are 'ordinarily' living — to qualify for residence — with owning a house being one sign of this, or just being there. In any case, the rules allow that you can visit your own, or any other country for up to 182 days even during this first year — or perhaps an average of less days over a longer period of time.

You can still travel around or go home to visit any time, if your visa situation allows. There is no problem about this

Also, temporary workers pay tax too — and you should look into claiming this back. Wherever you go, when you start work, you will pay tax on your income there, for things like social security and health, from day one. But there may be somewhere you can make an inquiry for a refund. All of which might seem like an unnecessary layer of bureaucracy . . . But can work to your advantage. And you might even be entitled to both sets of tax allowances in both countries if you are there for a short time

Residency and the Rolling Stones 5.22

Ah, here they are . . . The question of residency applies even if it is your own original country you are returning to. The *Rolling Stones* rock group came across a problem like this not so long ago when they had to postpone a concert in London after some tax changes — because they would have been in the UK too long during that year — the new rule was that being in the country for 'over an average of ninety days a year over five years' would make them residents of *Britain* for tax purposes.

Something they were not prepared to do. If they had come back then, the tax authorities in the UK *would have wanted to tax their worldwide income, not just the money they made from the concert*

Double taxation agreements 5.23

Otherwise, if there is a double taxation agreement between the two countries, money arising in that country is only taxable in that place — and any other income you may have there, like rent from property or the profits from a business.

As mentioned previously, keeping a record of pay slips, and bank statements, and tax and social security numbers and offices, is a very important thing you can do

Some personal advice 5.24

Talking to someone who has recently been there will be useful, from many angles, and getting some personal advice. One good way in *Britain* would be to contact *Corona Worldwide* (c/o The Commonwealth Institute, Kensington High Street, London W8 6NQ, UK; tel / fax 0207-610 4407; e-mail hq@corona.ww.prestel.co.uk; *www.commercepark.co.uk/corona*). They also have international contacts and connections — so you could contact them from your country about similar associations for emigrants or returned expatriates where you are . . .

"For almost fifty years we have been preparing people for a life in a country they know little about. In that time our style has changed — to keep pace with changing times. But essentially the basic anxieties and questions remain the same."

"We can fill the gaps through arranging a meeting with someone who has recently lived or worked in the country where you are going, or through our series of publications — 'Notes for Newcomers' *— each one full of practical information."*

"Corona Worldwide has branches and contacts in many countries throughout the world and networks with other associations with international interests. Through these we can usually provide you with a contact who will be willing to show you the ropes."

Notes for Newcomers 5.25

At present, the 'Notes for Newcomers' briefing notes cover what to take, what is available in the local shops, what services exist there (medical, recreational and others) what security and health precautions to consider; and also they can *"focus ideas before meeting a briefer when discussion can range more widely over areas of special interest or concern."*

There are three types of these meetings, or briefings, which they can arrange: a 'One Day Briefing' — "*with a financial adviser in the team, and if necessary someone with nursing experience;*" a 'Cultural Briefing' — "*with the briefer*" — at Corona's headquarters or elsewhere — "*suiting those who already have overseas experience. It is also suitable for the particular slot in the wider briefing which your company might offer;*" or there is a 'Telephone Briefing' — "*for those going at very short notice*" — a useful service.

Other leaflets they have include Culture Shock!, Living in a Muslim Country, Chinese Etiquette and Customs, *and* Returning to Britain.

F*or more background information and research about living and working in the country,* English Contacts Abroad — *PO Box 126, Oxford OX2 6AU, UK — can provide a full service of information and respond to your inquiries about the tax system as well as visas, trade, travel, immigration, travel and employment in over 100 countries: the fee being £48 /$80, individuals and organizations.*

Or email the author at Jonathan_Packer@hotmail.com

And see the Personal Experiences *of people who have lived and worked abroad in Appendix 1*

What to take and what to get there 5.26

Few countries do *not* have supermarkets and similar stores; but it might be worth going into one you know shortly before your trip — short-term or long — to get some small items to take — see *Getting there* and *Settling in* — like basic medicines, a supply of food — yes, do take some — and those items which might be more expensive on arrival. Some of these will be a better buy when you get there — and you would be the only one taking wine *into France* for instance, or second-hand cars *out* of *Russia*.

There is more about what to take in the chapters on Getting there *and* Settling in, *and the rest of this book; and much more you can find out about the country yourself under the headings of* Culture, Education *and the* Language, *which are useful subjects to think about now*

Read all about it 5.27

Also read up on the background — and your own interests — and see how they are part of life in that place — and see some travel books about the journeys others have made before which may help you now. Then there are all the facts, figures and statistics your investigations can provide.

Unfortunately, the older guidebooks are, the more misleading they can be. But a real travel book gets better with age. Find some of these in your library or local bookstore.

As do the books and the literature which come from that place — stories from *inside* that country or culture, like the book of short stories *Dubliners* and others by James Joyce, which are in part about the country he left behind — *Ireland*. As one example.

A travel book, a novel, fact or fiction . . . Books — and the art — movies — architecture — and music — originating in a country can be universal — and local too. So you might read Milan Kundera — another exile — coming from the Czech Republic, *Czechoslovakia as it was; or Tolstoy — if you have the time — or Chekhov or Dostoevsky from* Russia; *or Endo, Murakami or Maruya for* Japan

You can also look under Travel books *in* Sources of Information *for some more examples of books you could take*

The post office and its services 5.28

Post offices have many services you need — before you go and when you get there — from money transfer and *bureaux de change* to leaflets for health and insurance, and what to do about the post. In the *UK*, even small ones have this wide range of services — and leaflets on everything from driving licences to insurance. This makes them, along with libraries and your local shopping centre, a very useful, if undramatic, place to go. And when you get there

For the uninitiated, real mail not e-mail gets sent from here. Few yet have internet terminals — but 'cybercafés' and some shops do.

As the leaflet says,"*Relax, you can get everything at the Post Office.*" Here is a list of their services in the *UK*, which will be broadly similar to those in other places:

Bureaux de Change *—for 30 currencies, and traveller's cheques. They can buy back unused currency without commission*

Travel insurance *— for annual, multi-trip policies — or tel 0800-387 858*

Passport Application Service — *"We'll happily check and send your application and documents to help you avoid any last minute hitches in getting your passport"*

Form E111 *—for health on holiday in the European Union — "not a substitute for travel insurance"*

Royal Mail Keepsafe *— to arrange to have your mail delivered to you on your return*

Film Processing *— or this might be at your local photo shop*

BT Global card *— "to keep in touch with friends and family while you're away"*

Other international phonecards you can get would be useful, for phoning home. How much would postage be from that country? The answer is quite simply something similar to the rate for sending letters there

International Reply Coupons 5.29

Are exchangeable for stamps when you send an inquiry abroad, by the person you are sending it to. You can buy these in your local post office.

Or enclose a self-addressed envelope. Also see Letters abroad 2.33 *under* 6.Colleges and universities *in the list of ways to get a job abroad in the* Getting a job *chapter. Having some stamps to the right value from that country — or taking some when you go abroad when you go — will be useful*

Money transfer services 5.30

Western Union is available in over 100 countries, from *Albania* to *Zimbabwe;* and they will probably have a number where you are. There is a commission, but you can send cash almost anywhere like this; it is then available to be collected at any one of its outlets there, in about twenty minutes. They also issue their own advice about travelling abroad.

"*When you get home,*" they recommend, "*if you've been on a course of anti-malaria tablets, to complete the course, and report any flu-like symptoms to your doctor.*" Also "*check all your credit and charge card bills carefully. Your number may have been used fraudulently or you may have been charged for items you did not buy" — from their leaflet* 'World Travel Tips.'

Western Union: *UK Freephone 0800-833 833; Ireland Freephone 1800-395395;* www.westernunion.com

Other services 5.31

In any high street or shopping mall, you can find the post offices, travel agents, pharmacies and supermarkets you need . . . and in our more global economy this is a phenomenon you can find almost anywhere, from Waikiki to Warsaw . . . The retail industry is now 'global.' And many goods — such as books for instance — can be ordered and sent almost anywhere in the world. Or flowers . . . meaning it is just as cheap to buy quite a few items like this on the spot. You can buy them anywhere.

So you don't need to take everything with you, just the essentials of life

Language courses 5.32

You will meet new ways of life, and different customs; and you are going to need to learn at least some of the language — this is an un-voidable problem — or opportunity. The *Colloquial* series might be available in your library — with books and cassettes on:

Albanian, Amharic; Arabic (Levantine); Arabic of Egypt; Arabic of the Gulf and Saudi Arabia; Basque; Bulgarian; Cambodian; Cantonese; Chinese; Croatian and Serbian; Czech; Danish; Dutch; Estonian; Finnish; French; German; Greek; Gujarati; Hindi; Hungarian; Indonesian; Italian; Japanese; Korean; Latvian; Lithuanian;Malay;Norwegian;Panjabi;Persian;Polish;Portuguese;

Portuguese of Brazil; Romania; Russian; Slovak; Slovene; Somali; Spanish; Spanish of Latin America; Swedish; Thai; Turkish; Ukrainian; Vietnamese; Welsh

You need the cassette too; the price will be from £20 to £40. Call UK 0207-842 2098. Or you can find them at www.routledge.com

Doing your research 5.33

You need to know how banks and taxation work; and also the regulations for foreigners — and the health service, emergency numbers, immigration and emigration rules, importing and exporting, and so on — hours for shopping — bank holidays — and about a wide variety of other matters.

Where can you find out about all this? There are three main sources of information which are most useful when you are intending to live in a new country, far away from your usual sources of support — and which should be accessible to you wherever you are:

Their ***embassy*** or ***consulate*** can tell you more about business and work there; and the practical side of immigration, visas and work and / or residence permits

Where to go to find out more about living in the country is their ***tourist office*** — the one where you are — or one you can write to — which exists to spread the good news about this place as a tourist destination; but really can provide useful information on all aspects of life

And the third source of information is ***people***, those who have already lived and worked or are living there

To sum up — tax and residence 5.34

For tax and residence, the consulate of that country — where you are — or the local police station / town hall / or employer on the spot, can make these arrangements for you. This should be your first place to go. This seems like a technicality; but you need it.

What really counts, though, is your tax situation then, after you have done this, which you should check up on. It may well be — in some fortunate places like *Saudi Arabia* — that some grades of foreign workers work tax free, which simplifies matters. You then just have to square this with the tax authorities back home.

But think carefully about leaving this kind of tax-free job before the end of your contract, before your year is up, a full tax year in your own country, otherwise you may be liable to pay tax when you get home

By subscribing to the excellent **Overseas Jobs Express** *newspaper (Premier House, Shoreham Airport, West Sussex BN43 5FF, UK; tel 01273-440220/01273-440540; fax 01273-440229; e-mail editor@ overseasjobs.com;* www.overseasjobs.com*) you can also find out more about issues like this, and people who have already lived and worked abroad, and the experiences they had*

Healthcare 5.35

Questions to ask your local GP — when you go and ask for a check-up and vaccinations — or any health advice services offered by advice lines and travel clinics — are:

1. Does this country have a reciprocal healthcare agreement with my own?

2. *Are my national insurance or social security payments which I have made in my own country recognized there?*

In a country with no reciprocal healthcare agreement you really do have to get insurance — unless perhaps the local system is so generous as to treat all visitors needing emergency treatment for free.

Prepare for the worst, and then you can enjoy the best of your stay. So check — and see the *Getting there* and *Settling in* chapters for more on this — on the vaccinations you need; and sort out the basic medical kit you need to take; and have a dental check-up. Find out the telephone numbers for emergencies.

In the case of *Britain*, there are no reciprocal healthcare agreements with some pretty important places, like *Canada*, the *USA*, *India*, and many in the Far East, as well as nearly the whole of Africa and Latin America.

Visitors from these places too — to places like Britain and the United States — as well as the other way around — should ask about reciprocal healthcare agreements

Living in the USA 5.36

An extract from *Exodus* — the *Careers Europe Database of Careers Information*:

Income tax. *Income taxes in the* United States *can be levied by the US government (federal taxes), the state, and by municipalities. It is very important for foreign nationals to establish their status of residence as this has major implications for tax purposes — see* Working abroad *on* Legisation *and* Tax. *Resident aliens and non-*

resident aliens are taxed differently, with US residents taxed on their income worldwide, and non-US residents taxed on their US earnings only. Further evidence is available from the US Embassy, or the International Revenue Service (IRS)

Health Insurance. *Personal medical insurance in the* United States *is the responsibility of the individual, as there is no general state health provision. Many employers will give advice and financial assistance, but the cost of medical insurance is high, which reflects the high cost of medical fees.*

It is vital, therefore, for those travelling or moving to the United States *to ensure that they have adequate provision. Foreign nationals working there should also be aware of the totalization agreement which aims to ensure payments are not made into the social security funds of two countries. Further information in the* UK *from the* DSS Overseas Benefits Agency.

The Benefits Agency, Pensions and Overseas Benefits Directorate, Department of Social Security, Tyneview Park, Whitley Road, Benton, Newcastle-upon-Tyne NE98 1BA, UK; tel 0191-218 7777; fax 0191-228 7077

Department of Labor, Office of Public Affairs, 200 Constitution Avenue, NW, Room S-1032, Washington DC 20210, USA; tel +1-2-2-219-8211

Internal Revenue Service (IRS), Philadelphia Service Center, W-7 Unit, PO Box 447, Besalem PA 19020, USA; *www.irs.gov*

For people livng abroad, this UK database, run by the OPU *— see below — for* Eures *— the Europe-wide network for employment services in all the EU states — might also tell you about* Colleges *and* Further Education, Universities, Health, Pensions *and* Social Security, Taking a year out, *and give other contacts for* Cultural Organizations *in the* European Union / EEA *countries; and for work as well as living around the world*

Contact Eures *at the* OPU — Overseas Placing Unit, *Level 1, Rockingham House, 123 West Street, Sheffield S1 4ER, UK; tel 0114-259 6051; fax 0114-259 6040*

Taking care 5.37

Is what you need to do. The same applies to any transaction you are involved in, like buying a house when you don't know the local planning rules for instance.

Very often there will be an office helping local people draw up documents or make house purchases — even, for internatinal residents, a *Foreign Residents' Office* in places like *Spain* — and maybe another official who needs to authorize or notarize these official forms. These can help.

Or offices of lawyers speaking your language, or specializing in helping those from your community or other countries living there, for anything from business to important purchases you make. These might be a good contact, or valuable ally.

It will help having some contacts like these. And maintaining some connections with the community of people from your country who are living there. There will usually be some

And avoid illegality. That moustachioed stranger asking you to take consignments of cash out of the country knows the legal system there better than you do. Believe me

Buying property 5.38

A look around the neighbourhood will help you get a taste of the atmosphere; check out the shops, schools and transport like buses / trains / airports; and look at the place more than once, at different times of day, or on a weekday or weekend. Are the windows open? Are there any other suspicious signs like fresh paint suggesting there may be a problem being covered up? Or cracks in the wall or leaking guttering? What state is the woodwork in? Is that path up to the front door really your right of way (or belong to some aged local who will plague you for the rest of your stay)? Is the roof sound?

Discuss these points with your family / colleagues / friends . . . and if in doubt, draw up a list, of the good and bad ones. And buy in one transaction if you can — or you might prefer to do this in the currency where your income and funds are coming from, to avoid exchange rate variations. Or you might even get a mortgage in your own country even in the local currency — another way.

You can buy a house almost anywhere in Europe these days in euros. But better not to make the purchase a gamble on the exchange rate. And I would contact a local agency there.

If in doubt get some more advice or a second opinion; and don't be hurried into buying when you are not quite sure

A look around 5.39

On a preliminary trip you will get to know all these things more closely, if you go there to do some looking around, to get a job or find somewhere to live; or explore ways of starting a business; or visit some properties; finding out about healthcare, the education system, your new colleagues . . . all these things can be done.

The general rule is the more you know now the less you will have to worry about later on

What would it be like living in another country? 5.40

Is there some experience you can reflect on now — in your education, or in the workplace — where you achieved something you felt proud of, and which you felt was worthwhile — which could be one a way of understanding who you are now and your way of dealing with the world?

Maybe in relation to travel, or meeting people from different countries, or learning another language . . . all useful experiences to have.

Think about this. And how you relate to other people. It is your relationships with others — the people you know, and the ones you may meet on the way — which will be the most important part of your trip anywhere.

And on any journey. What is it that makes you happy or unhappy? What can make you proud — or its opposite, a feeling that you haven't achieved much? You can think about your past experience — as a way of understanding who you are now.

This is how this book started and how it ends. What will it be like living and working in another country? Or just travelling around, and spending some time there? This is an open-ended question.

The answer begins with you

5.41 Sources of information

Here are some places you can find out more about living and working abroad:

Your country's embassy / consulate locally
Their Home Office / Ministry of the Interior / Department of State
Their embassy / information centre before you go
Tourist offices locally / nationally
Local newspapers / magazines / guides
People from your country
People from that country
People from your country who live there
Friends and family
Acquaintances and colleagues
People you meet in and outside work
Ministries of Finance, Employment, Education, Health, Tourism, Trade and Industry...
Your local doctor
Your local tax office
Your local bank
Your local college / university
Trade associations and consultancies
International schools
Property agencies
Travel agencies
Cultural organizations and centres
Churches / religious organizations

Key Points

You can consider all the many sources of advice and information contained in this book, from A almost to Z . . . the advice also of friends and family, and think about what you want to do, now and in the future. But it still depends on you

Please return this questionnaire to:

Jonathan Packer, 'Living and Working Abroad', PO Box 126, Oxford OX2 6UB, UK

Your name: *age:* *profession:*

What did you do before going abroad?

When and where did you go?

How did you get a job there?

How about working there? How easy is it to adapt?

How easy is it to mix with people? What kind of social life is there?

What good or bad points about life in that country did you find?

What about travelling around? Do you have any tips or advice?

What were living conditions and accommodation like?

Bureaucracy and red tape? Were these a problem?

And the cost of living? Do you have any money-saving tips?

How did you prepare? What do people need to know before they go?

Please feel free to attach any longer answers to these questions; or anything else on residence and entry, accommodation, banks and taxation, health and insurance, and the employment scene generally

*This page may be photocopied **x 142 % / 1.42** to produce an A4 page*

All contributions will be acknowledged and are gratefully received

Last-minute news . . .

p.172 The Malaca Instituto (c/Cortada 6, 29018 Malaga, Spain, espanol@malacainst-ch.es. "For details of our quality guarantees please look up wwweaquals.org." General intensive Spanish; Hispanic studies (Spanish heritage); Mini-group exec courses; Commercial Spanish; DELE exam preparation; Selectividad preparation; Spanish for retired people; high school and college group programmes. Contact: Bob Burger

Primary International Healthcare Limited, Springfield House, Springfield Road, Horsham, West Sussex RH12 2RG, UK; tel +44 (0)1403 225110; e-mail primaryih@aol.com.

"We offer a Platinum plan which is a worldwide cover plan, a Gold plan which covers clients in their country of residence only, a travel plan for when they travel in or out of their country of residence, a Crewcare plan which is a medical and travel plan for professional yacht crew and a Première and Première Plus plan which is a top-up of the French national health system . . ." Offices in the UK, Dubai and Hong Kong — and see p.128

Activity International (PO Box 7097, 9701 JB Groningen, The Nertherlands, tel +31 (0)50-31 30 666, fax 31 31 633). They don't employ au pairs direct but do offer au pair stays, working holidays and exchanges for young Dutch people abroad, or people going to live there — info@activity.aupair.nl

More Property Abroad services: Cedric Mitchell Architects — e-mail 106235.2345@compuserve.com. World Class Homes, worldclasshomes@dial.pipex.com; apartments and properties in Catalonia and Spain

Direct Contacts

Appendix 1

Direct contacts for people intending to live and work abroad

All these contacts are not to be taken as a recommendation in any legal, financial or any other sense. The author regets that although every reasonable precaution is taken, no responsibility can be taken for any other service offered through these pages. Readers are advised to take all the necessary precautions before entering into any arrangement with organizations cited or prescribed in these pages. Take care!

Having said that, many of the following are known to me; others have been recommended — or recommended themselves; and seem reliable.

Nothing whatever in this book is true. Trust nobody (my final disclaimer — if you do end up on an alligator farm in El Salvador, fighting the crocs, for a morsel of dry bread at the end of each laborious working day, under that burning tropical sun, well don't blame me!

Here are, as I have said, some direct contacts for anyone interested in work, education, travel and employment anywhere in the world:

English Contacts Abroad (SEI, PO Box 126, Oxford OX2 6UB, UK) is an advice service for people looking for English-language teaching jobs abroad, with information, a background dossier and contacts for 'organizations recruiting now.' See the *ECA* questionnaire after the chapter *Working abroad.* A fee of £48 / $80 is charged.

Also for businesses setting up operations abroad

An international recruitment agency

Management recruitment and selection group *Michael Page International* has 55 offices in 12 countries and *"supports candidates as well as liaising with employers."* They also have *Michael Page Online* where you can submits CVs and search for vacancies (Source: *Smart Moves — Independent on Sunday* supplement; 1 Canada Square, London E14 5DC, UK; tel 0207-293 2222; *www.independent.co.uk*). *Also see* 2.22

Voluntary Service Overseas

Voluntary Service Overseas (tel 0208-780 1331, fax 0208-780 1081, e-mail enquiries@vso.org.uk, *www.oneworld.org/vso* — 317 Putney Bridge Road, London SW15 2PN, UK) says it is experiencing a rise in applicants, especially in areas like healthcare and nursing. Presently it has 1,700 people abroad in over 60 countries. And see *Personal Experiences — The Health Worker*

Overseas Jobs Express

Overseas Jobs Express (Premier House, Shoreham Airport, Sussex BN43 5FF; tel 01273 440220; fax 01273-440229; e-maileditor@overseasjobs.com; *www.overseasjobs.com*)

Its 'JOBS' columns include high-level and technical work like computing and consultancy through to seasonal work like skiing and summer camps — advertising for these seasonal ones starts about six months before.

There are regular features like 'News You Can Use'; an internet column; news about immigration / emigration for places like the *USA, Canada, New Zealand, Australia, South Africa,* and the European Union (and the *UK*); some more unusual ideas for work abroad — like being a movie extra — and the strange tales of people who have themselves have worked in a foreign land. The editor is Daniel James.

It is the model of its kind — the editor also answers queries on a living-and-getting-a-job-abroad problem page — with features on all aspects of living abroad from health to insurance — as well as being the best reference for getting a job anywhere in the world — for engineers, English teachers . . . and with an internet link-up remarkably described by publisher David Creffield as a *"Partner tool, which supports job-hunters in their search for work"* to many employment websites around the world:

"You can purchase batches of country and business specific address labels so you can mail off that newly prepared CV to the appropriate companies and agencies"

Newspaper advertising

The Guardian: **www.jobsunlimited.co.uk.** *'The Guardian* ***Appointments Diary:*** *Monday,* ***Media*** */ New* ***Media Guardian, Creative, Media*** *and* ***Sales, Marketing*** *and* ***PR, Courses, Secretarial 'Office Hours;'*** *Tuesday,* ***higher education, Senior, Universities, Research,*** *HE* ***Colleges,*** *General HE,* ***Courses***

— education, Senior, FE Colleges, General Education, Schools, TEFL, Courses; Wednesday, society, Senior, Health, Housing, Environment, General Public, Society Finance, Social Care, Volunteers, Courses, Agencies; Thursday, online, IT & T, IT Graduates, Courses, Science, Science & Technology; Saturday, Jobs & Money, General, Courses, rise:, Next move for graduates

***Just the Job** — Evening Standard.* supplement of the London *Evening Standard* newspaper published on Mondays: Northcliffe House, 2 Derry Street, London W8 5TT, UK; e-mail *justthe job@standard.co.uk;www.BigBlueDog.com)*with adverts, articles, news and contacts

Smart Moves is the ***Independent on Sunday*** supplement about management and careers: 1 Canada Square, London E14 5DC, UK; tel 0207-293 2222; fax 0207-293 2505 (to request a copy for advertising purposes); ***www.independent.co.uk*** — for UK jobs. They also have a section entitled presently 'Real Work'

Many of these newspapers are now on-line — all over the world — but not always their ads. The advertising section for air fares in the ***Telegraph*** newspaper on Saturdays is called 'Departure Gate': to advertise tel 0207-531 3004; fax 0207-538 6832; or to request a copy for advertising purposes. They have a 'Travel News' section. The travel editor is Roger Boynton

TNT magazine — is *"your guide to free spirited living"* (14—15 Child's Place, Earls Court, London SW5 9RX, UK; tel 0207-373 3377; faxlines 0207-341 6630 (editorial); 2440020/0050 (advertising);3416600(general enquiries);enquiries@tntmag.co.uk: mainly for those working in Britain — Australians, New Zealanders, South Africans, but also working travellers — or travelling workers — from anywhere — with many useful *UK* job and international travel contacts.

Also London accommodation, arts and entertainment listings, and flights

Your ***local press or national newspapers.*** These are probably the place to find out more and look for work around the world, even in your country

Student and college publications often have interesting travel and work-abroad articles

Your own direct contacts can be made through all the organizations and places mentioned at the end of Chapter 5 — like chambers of commerce, trade associations, embassies and tourist offices — for a list of these see Sources of Information

A book on languages

A Mouthful of Air — language and languages, especially English, Anthony Burgess, Hutchison, 20 Vauxhall Bridge Road, London SW1V 2SA, UK; also see 4.14

A book about travelling around the world

Race for the World by John Todd, Hodder Headline, London, *www.hodder.co.uk;* his story of being the first person to visit *"every country in the world, and the world's most travelled man."*

And see *Personal Experiences — The Traveller*

A list of recruitment agencies

The Expat Network Contact Directory has *"500 key recruiters for overseas jobs,"* a list of international recruitment agencies in a variety of fields. Contact: *Overseas Jobs Express*; 24-hour credit card hotline 01273-454522; e-mail betty@overseasjobs.com — and see also *Contacting companies* in *Getting a job* and under *Sources of Information*

A business travel agency

Smart BusinessTravel, Surrey Place, Mill Lane, Godalming, Surrey GU7 1EY, UK; tel 01483-419747; fax 01483-427030; e-mail contact@smartinformation.com — for travel bookers within companies and business travellers

Worldwide language schools

The Speak English School in Oxford. English in the 'city of dreaming spires,' famed for its university and cultural life . . .

The Speak English School offers courses for groups of university / high school and business students from all over the world, long-stay visitors, and special interest tours all across the UK like our 'B&Bs for Garden Visits' tour — looking after you during your stay. Please state your interest and requirements in your first inquiry. *"We look forward to meeting you."*

Contact: The Director, Speak English Schools, PO Box 126, Oxford OX2 6UB, UK

I.L.E.E. — programs in Argentina. *www.ilee.com.ar*

CLIC IH, Centro de Lenguas e Intercambio Cultural, c/ Albareda 19, 41001 Sevilla, Spain; telf +34 95 450 21 31; fax +34 95 456 16 96 — for Spanish, English, German and French; General Spanish, Business Spanish, Teacher Training, and a CELTA course for English language teachers, with cultural activities in and around the beautiful city of Sevilla

St. Giles Language Teaching Center, San Francisco. Full and part-time Cambridge RSA CELTA courses are offered by St. Giles in San Francisco — courses run by highly qualified and experienced trainers. *"Successful candidates can earn a graduate credit recommendation of six hours toward an MA TESOL."*

We also offer lifelong advice and assistance in finding work to our graduates. St. Giles Language Teaching Center, One Hallidie Plaza, San Francisco, CA 94102, USA; phone: (415) 788-3552; fax (415) 788-1923; email: sfstgile@slip.net; http://*www.stgiles-usa.com*

A freight company

Excess Baggage Company (London and national tel 0208-965 3344 - open 07.00 to 22.00; 168 Earls Court Road, London SW5, tel 0207-373 1977 — freephone 0800-783 9625 or 0800-783 1085; Paddington Station, Heathrow / Gatwick Airports; e-mail sales@excess-baggage.com; *www.excess-baggage.com*; fax 0208-961 2040) — can get your baggage *"anywhere"* by air/sea/road

A meeting service

Corona Worldwide has a meeting service for children at airports — see under *Websites* on the last page and also in previous chapters

Some removals firms

Over's International Removals has a *"full international service, and local knowledge. We have our own staff and facilities in most European countries and are experienced long-distance removers."* Address: Unit 8, Government Retail Industrial park, Government Road, Aldershot, GU11 2DA, UK; e-mail internationalrelocation @over.co.uk; tel 0800 24 34 33. Complete door to door service to all parts of the world

Lowes of Chester, 1 Hertford Way, Sealand Road, Chester, CH1 4NT, UK, tel 01244-373286, fax 01244-382575; Wirral: 0151-258 1558; Winsford 01606-331140. European and international removals, container storage, packaging — *"a complete service"*

Some publications about recruitment and business

Bradman's Business Asia (For frequent business flyers; published by Monomax; tel 0207-381 4442; fax 0207-381 8007) also *Bradman's Business Central Europe to Central Asia / Europe / Middle East / North / South America* — *www.bradmans.com.*

This Asia guide contains country overviews, airport to city centre transport information, orientation and getting around, conference venues, shopping, excursions, hotels, and nightlife

Interviewer magazine (*Inside Communications Ltd,* 9 White Lion Street, London N1 9XJ, UK; tel 0207-837 8727; fax 0207-837

7124) is for recruitment agencies in *Britain*, with jobs of this kind advertised — and news and features about careers. There is an annual trade fair which they organize, along with *FRES* (the *Federation of Recruitment and Employment Services* — also see under *Contacting companies / Recruitment agencies* in *Getting a job* and under *Career consultants and recruitment agencies* following) and *IEC* — with speakers and updates on issues affecting the recruitment industry.

The organizers' address is: Inside Communications Ltd, Bank House, 23 Warwick Road, Coventry CV1 2EW, UK; tel 02476-230333; fax 02476-252241

Magazines for travel

TNT magazine (14—15 Child's Place, Earls Court, London SW5 9RX, UK; tel 0207-373 3377; fax 0207-244 0050) — see above — also their *Australia and New Zealand Travel Planner* / websites

Wanderlust (PO Box 1832, Windsor, Berkshire SC4 6YP, UK; tel 01753-620426; fax 01753-620474). They have an annual travel writing competition; some destination reports on more out-of-the-way places; articles on practical travel matters — and sometimes on working abroad

E-magazine

Traveller's World (UK travel and accommodation guide; Peter Welham; tel 01865-242709; fax 01865-793162; £48 per year) *www.cpoint.co.uk*

Exhibitions

For details of *The Independent* newspaper's recruitment fairs, contact Tom Nelson (on his mobile): 0207-323 4469/4564

recruitment — organized by *Interviewer* magazine — see above under *Some publications about recruitment and business.* An annual recruitment exhibition for recruitment professionals

At ***Independent Traveller's World*** there are all kinds of tours, talks, expeditions and gadgets as I recall; tel 0207-341 6682 or 0800-328 0888 — in London and other *UK* cities like Glasgow, Manchester, Bristol. They sometimes ask recently returned / arrived travellers to act as unpaid 'Travel Guides' and give advice. Some agencies offering English teaching and other kinds of work, like summer camps and conservation, are here: *Independent Traveller's World*, 14 — 15 Child's Place, London SW5 9RX, UK

The ***World Travel Market***, also in Earls Court, London (head office: Oriel House, 26 The Quadrant, Richmond, Surrey TW9 1DL, UK; tel 0208-910 7981; fax 0208-334 0555; e-mail @reedexpo.co.uk) is the place to be — where you might find out more about the worldwide travel industry: and where the travel agents, tour operators and their various service providers meet.

Here, travel meets those who publicize it — with many destinations and their tourism representatives — of interest to journalists and researchers, and anyone. Open to the public on the busier Wednesdays and Thursdays, I would recommend a trip on the quieter Monday or Tuesday, open to its 'Meridian Club' members only, and the press.

World Travel Market Hotline: 01462-620222.

Also, their useful exhibition catalogue has many travel contacts;

published by *Showtime Media Sales*, Commerce House, 6 Grove Road, Hitchin, Herts. SG5 1SE, UK; tel 01462-422694; fax 01462-440707; e-mail showtimemedia@compuserve.com

For more worldwide travel trade fair and exhibition contacts see the Sources of Information *section which follows*

Bookstore

The Traveller's Companion mail order bookshop: tel 01463-233880. A recorded message. Leave a message and they will send you their extensive catalogue of maps and guides

The Open University

The *OU* is a distance-learning university in Britain and around the world — *"for people who want to make a difference to their lives."* And also Europe's *"biggest online university."*

"Whether you want to advance your career or change it, study at university level for the first time or pursue a personal interest in more depth, the OU can help."

Courses in: *arts; business and management; computing; education; health and social welfare; modern languages; English law; mathematics; psychology; science; social sciences; environment;* and *technology.*

And there are regional centres around the world. Contact: *The Open University*, PO Box 625, Milton Keynes MK7 6AA, UK; hotline (24 hours): 0870-858585; *www.open.ac.uk/brochure/*

"More information can be obtained by calling 01908-858585;

or writing to the OU, PO Box 625, Walton Hall, Milton Keynes MK7 6AA, UK; or for more information about language courses tel 0870-900 0302; also www.Open2.net"

Also see the 'A — Z of jobs abroad' in Working Abroad, 1.6, *and the section on* TV *in* Settling in, 4.21

We will be pleased to include further information on international schools, language courses, language schools and travel agencies in future issues — and all organizations and suppliers of services, from language schools to recruitment agencies, of interest to readers. Please write or send your information to:

Jonathan Packer, Living and Working Abroad, PO Box 126, Oxford OX2 6UB, UK; or *Jonathan_Packer@hotmail.com*

Our aim is to include the right information for people living, working, travelling, studying and doing business anywhere in the world'

Career consultants and recruitment agencies

The pages of a publication such as *Overseas Jobs Express* will reveal there are many agencies for work in very many countries which specialize in work abroad — or see *www.overseasjobs.com* . Or the *Expat Network Contact Directory*, tel 0208-760 5100

See under *Contacting companies*, 2.19; and *International recruitment agencies*, 2.22, where there are just a few of the many international recruitment agencies which exist. Also Chambers of Commerce — 2.13 — and employment services — 2.9, 2.10, 2.11.

Or contact *FRES* — the *Federation of Recruitment and Employ-*

ment Services: tel 0207-323 4300; 36-38 Mortimer Street, London W1N 7RB, *UK;* tel 0207-323 4300. They can be contacted for lists of their members offering jobs overseas, or agencies offering work in particular areas, which they can send a list of for a small fee — or consultants who advise on careers.

Career World, Tong Hall, Tong BD4 0RR, UK; tel 0800-731 7237 24-hour freephone; fax 0113-285 4556; e-mail aw@career-world.co.uk; *www.career-world.co.uk*

"A leading career management and outplacement consultancy with offices throughout the UK and Europe. Call for a free and confidential exploratory meeting at a location near you"

RWH International Inc: www.CanadaUSemployment.com

The job you want . . . in the city you want.

Job offer attainment the professional way.

E-mail: info@canadausemployment.com

Tel: 001-416-636-3933 / Fax: 001-416-636-8113

A licensed international employment agency.

Proudly serving clients since 1995. Canada/USA

There are also consultants and advice services like these where you are — part of national employment services or privately — advising people on new jobs or careers they can have

Contacts for trade and industry

You should contact the embassy for details of joint chambers of commerce. And your national or local business organizations and advice centres. These can be sources for details of trade and companies operating in that country, factsheets and leaflets, and rules and regulations for setting up a business; or for local chambers of commerce in the place you are going which are also worth contacting for example to find out about scholarships and work placements / internships, and even voluntary work.

These joint chambers of commerce exist to promote trade between the two countries — see earlier in *Getting a job* under this heading at 2.13. Some of these also produces newsletters and updates, for example the *Russo-British Chamber of Commerce*, 42 Southwark Street, London SE1 1UN, UK, tel 0207-403 1706, fax 0207-403 1245 — and organize events and conferences for exporters and businesspeople — and have businesses as their members.

There might also be other trade offices you can contact:

ICEP (Investment Trade and Tourism of Portugal), 22-25A Sackville Street, London W1X 1DE, UK; tel 0207-494 1441; fax 0207-494 1441 — at the same address as the Portuguese tourist office — but on a different floor . . .

Latin American Trade Advisory Group, Canning House, 2 Belgrave Square, London, UK SW1X 8PJ; tel 0207-235 2303; fax 0207-259 6962, e-mail 1061665.1317@compuserve.com

The *East European Trade Council — EETC*, Suite 10, Westminster Palace Gardens, Artillery Row, London SW1P 1RL, UK — tel 0207-222 7622, fax 0207-222 5359 — has a library very useful for research — this is an organization attached to the *dti* — see the following page — and at *www.eetc.org.uk*

Also contact:

your ***Ministry of the Economy / Department of Trade and Industry.*** This ministry will also organize conferences, trade fairs and trade missions — tel 0207-215 5000 for the DTI in Britain: *www.dti.gov.uk*

Embassies. *These will have a counsellor or representative responsible for commerce, so contact this person too.*

For US embassies around the world contact the US Department of State, *www.state.gov: Washington, DC, 20520, tel 202-647-4000*

Business consultancies. *These are important in the area of trade, especially with new markets and developing countries. They are good sources and contacts for the tax system, rules and regulations for starting a business and employing staff, or to find out about companies operating there*

Chambers of commerce. *American Chambers of Commerce* (UK), 75 Brook Street, London W1Y 2EB; tel 0207-493 0381

Sources of Information

Appendix 2

Where to find out more about living and working abroad

Consider your family, friends, colleagues at work or people you have met while travelling . . . All of these can be useful sources of support.

Books about living and working abroad

Straightforward Publishing, 38 Cromwell Road, London E17 9JN, UK, publishes books about your life and life choices, employment, business and travel including the following forthcoming titles:

A Straightforward Guide to Teaching English Around the World

A Straightforward Guide to Business Travel

A Straightforward Guide to Research on the Internet

And books about the *Law, Business, Childcare, Writing, Personal Development, Property, Driving,* and *General* titles — including *The Straightforward CV* (ISBN 1899924 — £6.99); and, for those going to live in the United Kingdom, *A Straightforward Guide to Your Rights as a Private Tenant* (ISBN 1899924 42 6 — £7.99), *A Straightforward Guide to Employment Law* (ISBN 1899924 65 5 — £7.99), *The Straightforward Business Plan* (ISBN 18999 24 40 0 — £7.99) and many others.

Straightforward Publishing:

Online at *www.straightforwardco.co.uk*

E—mail info@straightforwardco.co.uk

Sales@straightforwardco.co.uk

For trade and *UK* / international orders contact:

Turnaround Distribution, Unit 3, Olympia Trading Estate, Coburg Road, Wood Green, London N22 6TZ, UK; tel 020-8829 3000; fax 020-8881 5088; *orders@turnaround-uk.com*

For the *USA* / internationally contact: **Alliance House Inc**, 220 Ferris Avenue, White Plains, New York, 10603, USA, tel 914-328-5456, fax 914-946-1929, e-mail **info@alliancehouse .com** — also to order the 'international' edition of this book: 'Off the Beach — A Straightforward Guide to Living and Working Abroad'

You can contact the author direct at: PO Box 126, Oxford OX2 6UB, UK

The useful *Expat Network Contact Directory* has around 500 companies who are *"key recruiters for overseas jobs"* and is published annually (Contact *Overseas Jobs Express* 24-hour credit card hotline 01273-454522; e-mail betty@overseasjobs.com — to order this and many other books about living / working abroad)

Travel books

A Fortune-Teller Told Me — Earthbound Travels in the Far East, Tiziano Terzani, (Flamingo, 77-85 Fulham Palace Road, Hammersmith, London W6 8JB, UK) ISBN 0-00-655071-1 — gives a real insight into this region; also his *Goodnight, Mister Lenin* will tell you about the end of the Soviet Union, and a lot about Russia and Central Asia

Beyond Belief—Islamic Excursions among the Converted Peoples, V.S. Naipaul, (Abacus) ISBN 0-349-11010-7 — on *Indonesia, Iran, Pakistan* and *Malaysia*, and *"a book about people . . . not opinion."* Also see *An Area of Darkness, India: A Wounded Civilization* and *India: A Million Mutinies Now* on *India*; also his writings on the Caribbean, Latin America and elsewhere

Driving Over Lemons — An Optimist in Andalucía, Chris Stewart, (Sort Of Books / Penguin, PO Box 18678, London NW3 2FL, UK) ISBN 0-684-85802-9 — the not-quite rock star and first drummer of Genesis buys a remote farm in *Spain* — and writes this best-seller

The Hills of Tuscany, Ferenc Máté, Flamingo (HarperCollins Publishers, 77-85 Fulham Palace Road, Hammersmith, London W6 8JB, UK) ISBN 0-00-65592-0 — brings a more a more lyrical, poetic style to this tale of *Italy*

Running a Hotel on the Roof of the World — Five Years in Tibet, by Alec Le Sueur (Summersdale Publishers Ltd, 46 West Street, Chichester, West Sussex PO19 1RB, UK) ISBN 1-873475-93-4 — who spent five years running a hotel in *Tibet*. What's it like running the Holiday Inn in Lhasa?

The Seven Year Hitch — A Family Odyssey, David R. Grant (Simon and Schuster, Africa House, 64-78 Kingsway, London WC2B 6AH), ISBN 0-684-85802-9 — is about this journey circumnavigating the globe by horse-drawn caravan — with family

Under the Dragon — Travels in a Betrayed Land, Rory Maclean

(Flamingo—HarperCollins)—the betrayed land in question being *Burma*

Black Lamb and Grey Falcon — A Journey through Yugoslavia, Rebecca West (*Canongate Classics*, 14 High Street, Edinburgh, Scotland) ISBN 0-86241-428-8 — Her observations about the countries of former *Yugoslavia* are relevant today; and classic travel books can be a good companion on a trip to a strange land.

Eric Newby, *Jan Morris* and *Vitali Vitaliev* are some more recent travel writers who are interesting because of what they say, and the way they write — not just for clichéd accounts of their own adventures. *Departures and Arrivals* by Eric Newby (HarperCollins) contains snapshots of his life and travels. *Slowly Down the Ganges* is another one I enjoyed by him. His *The Big Red Train Ride* took him by Trans-Siberian Express across the USSR.

Novels can sometimes tell you as much about a country, sometimes much more than any guidebook. These can be by outsiders — like *A Room with a View* by E.M Forster. This story starts in Florence a century ago — giving the point of view of a traveller there, who wants to throw her guidebook away.

These are people on the outside looking in. Novelist Henry James can be like this too — and a glimpse of this somewhat stylized Jamesian world of late Victorian travel and life in grand hotels can still be had in some places.

The Beach by Alex Garland — set in *Thailand* — explores some of the same issues — of travel versus tourism — and the perils of a rootless adventure into the unknown — in the backpacking present day. Somewhere between adventure travel, and moving abroad. Now that major motion picture . . .

Travels through France and Italy (The World's Classics, Oxford University Press, Walton Street, Oxford OX2 6DP, UK) by Tobias Smollett takes us back to the eighteenth century, in the form of letters home during this real-life trip. He also wrote fiction; and his novels will give you a 'realistic' feel for travel at this time.

Fact or fiction? The boundary can be blurred in a highly fictionalized account like *A Sentimental Journey* by Laurence Sterne (first published in 1768) where it is the impressions in a very subjective way which count.

Travel, and living and working abroad, also go back in time — and are not just part of our modern experience — so a story like that of the medieval Italian traveller Marco Polo can be instructive — for anyone going abroad — and help to show how trade and the meeting of cultures have always been with us

An international book club is The Good Book Guide *which publishes a magazine and has regular updates on the latest books, videos, CDs and gifts — which can be mailed all over the world:* 24 Seward Street, London EC1V 3PB, UK

Software 'for leisure and learning' — everything from languages to games, Ordnance Survey and National Geographic maps and magazines, encyclopedias and databases — even a "powerfultext-based library of the world's classics, from antiquity to the 20th century" — *all these can be ordered from* Dream leisure and learning sofware: *www.eDREAM.co.uk, tel 01865-888900*

Guides and maps

Cartographia maps — H-1590 Budapest, POB 80, *Hungary*. I also found them, along with some other companies, on the Internet at *www.global-perspectives.com*

Central.America (budget.zone), by alexis de gheldere, *Ulysses Travel Publications* (4176 Rue Saint-Denis, Montréal, Québec, *Canada* H2W 2MS, *www.zone.qc.ca*, zone@zone.qc.ca) ISBN 2-89464-182-6 — a translation of their *Amérique centrale*, and a good guide for budget travellers; also *Stagiaires sans frontiéres* for those seeking internships or work placements abroad

DINAGECA, (Derecção Nacional de Geografia e Cadastro de Moçambique) Av. Josina Machel 537, CP 288, Maputo, *Mozambique*, tel 3025/55/6-1998

Footprint Handbooks, 6 Riverside Court, Lower Bristol Road, Bath BA2 3DZ, UK, tel 01225-469141, fax 01225-469461, e-mail handbooks@footprint.cix.co.uk / *Passport Books*, 4255 West Touhy Avenue, Lincolnwood (Chicago), Illinois 60646-1975, USA, tel 847-5500, fax 847-6792494, e-mail NTCPUB2@AOL.COM — a series of guides from Andalucía to *Vietnam*. Their *South American Handbook* was the winner of the Thomas Cook 'Best Travel Guide' award

Impact — specialist travel, career and business titles, 9104 Manassas Drive, Suite N, Manassas Park, Virginia 20111-5211, USA, tel 703-361-7300, fax 703-335-9486, *www. impactpublications. com*

Kümmerly & Frey maps — HE-3001, Bern, *Switzerland* — for Europe, its countries and regions, and the rest of the world

Michelin — the famous series of tourist and motoring atlases and guides: Place des Carmes-Déchaux 63, Clermont-Ferrand, *France*; or UK: 38 Clarendon Road, Watford, Herts WD1 1SX; tel 01923-415000; *www.michelin-travel.com*

Missing Maps, East View Cartographic Inc., 3020 Harbor Lane North, Minneapolis, MN 55447, USA; tel 612-694-9608; fax 612-559-2931; e-mail marc@eastview.com — for very rare or missing maps coming from Russia among other places, and a bookstore; Call US toll-free 0800-800-3839

The National Geographic Traveler series has books on *France*, *Britain*, *Canada*, Paris, New York, with illustrations, and also getting there by car and where to drive . . . *National Geographic Society*, 1145 17th Street N.W., Washington, D.C. 20036-4688, *www.nationalgeographic.com*. Also the famous magazine

Nelles maps — for all over the world, including Asia/Pacific and Latin America: *Nelles Verlag GmbH*, D-80935 München, *Germany*

"The world's largest map and travel bookshop" — is *Stanfords*, near Covent Garden and Leicester Square: 12-14 Long Acre, London WC2E 9LP, UK; tel 0207-836 1321; fax 0207-836 0189

Thomas Cook World Timetable—Independent Traveller's Edition (Thomas Cook Publishing, PO Box 227, Thorpe Wood, Peterborough PE3 6PU, UK, e-mail timetables@thomascook.com), ISBN 0-905802-08-X — this one has rail and bus services; and the other Thomas Cook rail timetables are useful too. I recommend also to contact local tourist offices

Travel Without Tears (Need2Know Guides)— see *Working Abroad* under *Travelling with your family* — sections on *'Travelling in*

pregnancy,' 'Travelling with a baby,' 'Travelling with a toddler,' 'Lone parents,' and other special circumstances

The world at your feet, Nina Hathway, Age Concern England, 1268 London Road, London SW11 4ER, UK — also see *Retirement* in the *A — Z of working abroad* in the *Working Abroad* chapter

World Leisure Marketing — distribution of maps and guides for just about anywhere, from a wide variety of sources: 9 Downing Road, West Meadows, Derby DE21 6HA, UK; tel 01332-573737; e-mail office@wlmsales.co.uk; *www.map-guides.com.* A tubed Hereford *MappaMundi,* or a street map of Hobart, Tasmania, they have it all . . .

World Travel Guide (*Columbus Press Ltd,* Jordan House, 47 Brunswick Place, London N1 6EB; fax 0207-250 4908/9) — 250 countries in accurate, up-to-date detail — as used by professionals, and an excellent, comprehensive source for embassies and tourist offices — now published on the web: *www.wtgonline.com*

The Virgin student travellers' handbook — the definitive guide to planning a 'gap year', Tom Griffiths, (*Virgin Publishing Ltd,* Thames Wharf Studios, Reinville Road, London W6 9HT, UK), ISBN 0-7535-0363-8 (UK) / 0-7627-0017-11 (USA) — relentlessly cheerful, with a forward by the entrepreneur Richard Branson

The *Royal Geographical Society* has a map room with an extensive collection of world maps; and you do not have to be a member — or fellow — to consult them — as you would often with the major university libraries. *Royal Geographical Society — Institute of British Geographers (RGS — IBG),* 1 Kensington Gore, London SW7 2AR, UK; tel 0207-591 3000; *www.rgs.org*

Magazines and other publications

Australia News, Canada News, Destination New Zealand, Going USA, and *Emigrate* are all published by *Outbound Newspapers*, 1 Commercial Road, Eastbourne, East Sussex BN21 3XQ, UK; tel 01323-726040; fax 01323-649249; e-mail outbounduk@aol.com — most edited by the ubiquitous Steve Hartridge. Useful for emigrants to these countries, with the basic facts and figures, and also commercial organizations you need. They organize an annual property abroad show at Sandown racecourse

Caribbean World (84 Albert Hall Mansions, Prince Consort Road, Knightsbridge, London SW7 2AQ, UK; tel 0171-581 9009; fax 0181-581 2279; e-mail@caribbeanworld.demon.co.uk; *www.caribbeanworld.demon.co.uk*) is a more upmarket, glossy type of magazine

The Expatriate (175 Vauxhall Bridge Road, London SW1 1ER, UK; tel 0207-233 8595; fax 0171-233 8718; e-mail 106044.1374@compuserve.com) editor: Vera Madam

Geographical is the magazine of the *Royal Geographical Society* — see above. Editorial address: 47c Kensington Court, London W8 5DA, UK; tel 0207-938 4011; fax 0207-938 4022; e-mail enquiries@geographical.co.uk.Subscriptionenquiries:POBox285, Sittingbourne, Kent ME9 8PF, UK; tel 01795-414881; fax 01795-414555;e-mail@galleon.co.uk

Home and Away (*Expats International Ltd*, Expats House, 29 Lacon Road, East Dulwich, London SE22 9HE, UK; tel 0208-299 4986; fax 0208-299 2484) editor: Keith Edwards

Living in France — The Regional Guide to France and French Lifestyle (see the following *Property* section)

Overseas (*Commonwealth Publishing Ltd*, New Zealand House, 80 Haymarket, London SW1Y 4TE, UK; tel 0207-747 9200; fax 0207-747 9223; e-mail nznlondon@aol.com / satimes@aol.com) — for those from New Zealand and elsewhere working in Britain

hr world (2—6 Northburgh Street, London EC1 0AY, UK) about 'managing the global workforce' and similar issues

human resources (22 Bute Gardens, London W6 7DR, UK; tel 0208-943 5000; fax 0207-413 4503) on employment and 'hrm'

People Management (17 Britton Street, London EC1M 5JP, UK ; tel 0207-880 6200; fax 0207-336 7637) human resources and personnel people again — leading me to wonder, by the way, if these are always the right people to contact in a company if you want a job there. Someone else, anyone — the boss, head of that department, the press/PR person — may be better

Adventure Travel (PO Box 6254, Alcester, Warwickshire, UK; tel 01789-488166; fax 01789-488462) features destinations from *Iran* to Irian Jaya — and you can send them an account of your adventures too

Editur — and *Editur Latinoamérica* (Juan Bravo, 46, 1°, 280006 Madrid, *Spain*; tel +34-91-309 20 53; fax +34-91-401 21 68; e-mail editur6@ibernet.com; *www.editur.es/latino*) is the main travel trade magazine in that country — and now for Latin America

Essentially America (*PhoenixPublishing*, 18—20 Scrutton Street, London EC2A 4TG, UK; tel 0207-247 0537; fax 0207-377 2741; e-mail postmaster@phoenix.wits.co.uk) — is for visitors and intending *USA* residents, a glossy guide

Guidelines (Profi Reisen Verlags.ges.m.b.H., Gaertnergasse 15,

1030 Vienna, *Austria*; tel +43-1 714 24 14; fax +43-1 714 24 14-4; *www.profi-reisen.co.at*, although I couldn't find them there). This is a travel magazine in German for tour guides

Language Travel Gazette (33 Riding House Street, London W1P 7PG, UK; tel 0207-436 3506; tel — for advertising — 0207-436 3514/5; fax 0207-436 3503; e-mail mail@languagetravel.com; *www.languagetravel.com*) — a magazine about language travel

Living in France — The Regional Guide to France and French Lifestyle (*Picture House Publishing Ltd*, 9 High Street, Olney, Buckinghamshire MK46 4EB, UK; tel 01234-713203; fax 01234-711507; e-mail livingfrance@easynet.co.uk; *www.livingfrance.com*) on finance and legal matters, as well as general interest articles and special reports about property there — see also *Travel Trade Fairs* below, and *'Vive La France'*

National Geographic is the *"official journal of the National Geographic Society;"* call 1-800-NGS-LINE toll free for *U.S., Canada* for information; 8 a.m. — midnight ET; Mon — Fri, 8.30 a.m. — 7 p.m. ET, Sat. Write: *National Geographic Society*, PO Box 98199, Washington, DC 20090-8199, USA, *www.nationalgeographic.com*

Nexus Expatriate Magazine (*Expat Network Ltd.*, International House, 500 Purley Way, Croydon CR0 4NZ, UK; tel 0208-760 5100; fax 0208-760 0469; e-mail:expatnetwork@demon.co.uk; *www.expatnetwork.co.uk*) has destination reports, articles about careers and jobsearching; their website is also — like many others — an on-line bookstore

Smart Business Travel — see 'A business travel agency' in *Direct Contacts* — tel 01483-419747 — for incentive travellers, and organizations sending staff abroad

Thomas Cook Magazine (7 St. Martin's Place, London WC2H 4HA, UK; tel 0207-747 0700; fax 0207-747 0701) — *"How to get the most from holidays and travel"*

Tour hebdo (tel +33-1 41 29 97 53; fax +33-1 41 29 97 95 — editorial; fax +33-1 41 29 97 93 — advertising) — is a travel trade magazine for agencies and tour operators in *France*

Transitions Abroad, P.O. Box 1300, Amherst, MA 01004-1300, USA; tel 413-256-3414; fax 413-256-0373; info@TransitionsAbroad.com — *TransitionsAbroad.com* — a bimonthly magazine about living, working, studying and traveling internationally, including information like a *Directory of ESL Training / Placement Programs, Volunteer* and *Internship Programs, Short-term* and *Volunteer Work Abroad,* and feature articles: *"Our readers — educated travelers of all ages and interests — rely on* Transitions Abroad *for their overseas work and travel plans"* — also their every-two-years guide to work abroad, called *Work Abroad*

Traveller **(*WEXAS International,* 45—49 Brompton Road, Knightsbridge, London SW3 1DE, UK; tel 0171-581 4130; fax 0207-581 1357) covers a range of interests and many destinations from a practical point of view. These WEXAS people run *"the UK's Premier Travel Club"* and *"a multinational travel association with 35,000 leisure and business travel members in nearly 100 countries."* You get 'Traveller' when you join - there are corporate membership and travel services for companies: tel 0207-589 3315; fax 0207-589 8418; *e-mail mship@wexas.com***

TravellingFreestyle— *www.flightbookers.net* — or *e.bookers.com* — Butler House, 177—178 Tottenham Court Road, London W1P 0LX, UK; tel 0207-757 2102; fax 0207-757 2200 — the magazine of the ticket agency

Travel Plus (21 Colebrooke Row, Islington, London N1 8AP, UK; tel 0207-359 7374; fax 0207-359 7375) *"the one-stop reference source full of today's innovative products and services for you the business traveller"*

Articles from *The Times* are on their internet site: *www.the-times.co.uk;* also the *TES (Times Educational Supplement)* and their on-line jobs; and a TES bookshop / library

The Economist magazine is available on the internet by 10pm London time on Thursdays:

25 St James Street, London SW1A 1HG, UK; tel 0207-830 7000; fax 0207-839 2968/9

and 111 West 7th Street, New York, NY 910019, USA; tel 212-541-0500; fax 212-541-9378

Property

Holiday (Kettering Parkway, Kettering, Northamptonshire NN15 6EI, UK; tel 01536-310101; fax 01536-414682) for timeshares — editor Brian Folley

International Homes (3 St. John's Court, Moulsham Street, Chelmsford, Essex CM2 0JD, UK; fax 01245-357767) from the USA to the Mediterranean

Interval (Illustrated London News Group, Sea Containers House, 20 Upper Ground, London SE1 9PF, UK) another for timeshares

World of Property — another publication of *Outbound Newspapers* (1 Commercial Road, Eastbourne, East Sussex BN21 3XQ, UK; tel 01323-726040; fax 01323-649249); and each year they organize a trade fair which boasts the *"largest display of property overseas in the UK"* at Sandown Park Racecourse, Portsmouth Road, Esher, Surrey — for *Spain, Florida, France, Portugal, Greece,* the *USA, Malta, Cyprus, Italy* and the *Canary Islands*

Leptos Esates: tel 0208-340 8096; fax 0208-341 4334; e-mail petros@leptos.demon.co.uk—property in *Cyprus* and a 'roadshow'

Olympic Holidays / Odyssey Holidays (0208-343 9090): *"the new brochure is highlighting a variety of special deals for early bookers which include substantial savings at more than 150 properties and a special low deposit of just £25." Interaction Ltd*: 1 Torrington Park, London N12 9SU, UK; tel 0208-343 7300; fax 0208-343 7444

Papillon properties is an experienced agency which has an excellent and recommended fact sheet / questionnaire; and a service providing properties *"from cottages to castles"* in the Mid Western Poitou-Charentes region of *France;* and can help through all stages of the buying process. UK Phone / Fax: 01279-771725; France: Phone +33-5-49-87-45-47; Fax +33-5-49-87- 51-99; e-mail papillon@mellecom.fr; *www.mellecom.fr/papillon*

Worldwide Property Consultants (01462-731846; e-mail sales@wwpc.uk.com). A consultancy offering over 6,000 properties in and outside Europe — employing usually bilingual staff

There will also be other similar roadshows and exhibitions in 'living abroad' publications and articles. *Also see p.166*

Going to the country itself will probably be the best way. And see the tips for Buying property *in* Living abroad — 5.38

Travel trade fairs

New ones are springing up all the time. The world of travel is changing — notably with the introduction of the Internet; and more holidays in more places which were previously difficult to get to, and where many more of us are likely to end up living and working in future.

http://travel.reedexpo.com is where *Reed Travel Exhibitions* is, on the world wide web. As well as the *World Travel Market* in London (see *Direct Contacts*) they organize the *British Travel Trade* fair for incoming tourism to the UK each spring, at the National Exhibition Centre in Birmingham: "*hotline: 01923-774883; fax 0208-910 7879.*" Events they organize are:

PATA (Pacific Asia Travel Association) TravelMart in *Singapore*; *Arabian Travel Market* in the *United Arab Emirates — Dubai* — for the Middle East; *EIBTM* — for *"meetingsandbusinesstravel"* — in Geneva; *American Travel Market* (usually September) in Orlando, Florida; *Greek and Balkan Travel Market* — for all the countries of the region — in Thessaloniki each November; TOURF — International Tourism Trade Fair for Holidays, Travel and Leisure in Salzburg, Austria; and their *CIS Travel Market* for the *Commonwealth of Independent States* in St. Petersburg.

For more about visiting or exhibiting contact *RTE* on fax 0208-910 7733 (their 'faxback' service); or at Oriel House, 26 The

Quadrant, Richmond, Surrey TW9 1DL, *UK*; tel 0208-910 7908; or Reed Travel Exhibitions, 383 Main Avenue, Norwalk, CT, 06851, *USA*; tel 203-840-5626; 1-800-363-3631; fax 203-840-9626; *www.reedexpo.com* — also for American Travel Market / ATM

independent traveller's world — see *Direct Contacts* previously

ITE Travel Exhibitions organizes *Holiday World* (for Central Europe, in Prague); *Emitt* (for the Eastern Mediterranean — in Istanbul); *Mitt* (in Moscow); *Uitt* (in Kyiv); Gulf (in Bahrain); and *Initt* (in New Delhi, *India*).

"To receive further information on how to exhibit at — or visit — any of these exhibitions — or Expotourisme *in Paris — contact* ITE Travel Exhibitions *on fax 0207-268 0177; e-mail: travel@ite-exhibitions;* www.ite-exhibitions.com/travel"

Brussels Travel Fair, Place de Belgique, B-1020 Brussels, *Belgium*; tel +32-2 477 04 77; fax +32-2 477 03 90 — each November

Tashkent International Tourism Fair — Tourism Along the Silk Road — is for the Central Asian tourism and travel markets — at the Uzexpocentre: Directorate Tashkent International Tourism Fair, 115 Buyuk Ipak Yuli satr., Tashkent, 700077, *Uzbekistan*; tel +3712-6867 75/77, 133 11 68; fax +3712-68 67 75, 139

The *European Tourism Trade Fairs Association (ETTFA)* is the *"voice of the travel exhibition industry"* — PO Box 79, Vilová 16, 100 31 Prague 10, *Czech Republic*; tel +42-02 671 00 100; fax +42-02 671 00 101; e-mail secretariat@ettfa.org; *www.ettfa.org*

Their *Tourism Exhibitions Directory* is *"the valuable tool that presents Travel and Tourism Exhibitions and Trade Fairs worldwide."* It will presently cost you $65 and is published by

Interbooks, 18 Ippokratous st., GR-10680 Athens, Hellas — it says here — e-mail tedpress@travelling.gr; *www.hellas-on-business.gr/ted*; tel +3013611716 / 3093343754 / 3094666427. It is in German, Italian, Greek, English and French. Author Theodore A. Koumelis has also produced 'Hellenic Tourism Myth and Reality'

Vive La France —French lifestyle and life, London Jan / Feb, Haymarket Exhibitions Limited, 'ticket hotline' tel 0121-767 4707

Employment and other exhibitions

LondonLanguageShow—products,servicesandideasforlanguage learning: organisers, *Brintex*, 32 Vauxhall Bridge Road, London SW1V 2SS, UK; tel 0207-973 6401; fax 0207-233 5054

The Postgraduate Study and Training Fair — January / February each year — tel 0800-252 183; or 0207-554 4540. Run by *The Guardian* and *The Observer* newspapers and the *University of London Careers Service*, a university careers service which also produces some useful leaflets, books and training videos

Skills and Employabilty for Graduates: a conference of interest to universities and professionals — organized in 2000 by *Neil Stewart Associates*, 13th Floor, Centre Point, 103 New Oxford Street, London WC1A 1DD, UK; tel 0207-240 9393; fax 0207-240-8833 — about skills and employability — along with the UK government's *Department for Employment and Education*

International tourist offices

National tourist offices will be in the Yellow Pages / business telephone directory for your capital city; or might be contacted through the embassy — and of course advertise their services too. Travel agencies could also put you in touch — and with local tourist offices around the world.

Here are some other national, regional and local tourist offices:

Alaska Division of Tourism, PO Box 110801, Juneau, Alaska 99811-0801, *USA*; tel 1-907 465 5478; fax 1-907 465 2287

Amazonas Tourist Board, Av 7 De Setembro, 1546 Vila Ninita, Manaus 69005-141, *Brazil*; tel +55-92 633 2983; fax +55-92 233 9973

Balearic Islands — IBATUR, Calle Montenegro 5, 07012 Palma de Mallorca, *Spain*; tel +34-971 17 71 50; fax +34 971 71 06 00 — *Menorca, Mallorca, Ibiza, Formentera*

Beijing Tourism Office, 28 Jianguomenwai Ave., 100022 Beijing, *China*: tel +86-10 6515 8844; fax +86 10 6515 8251

Brazilian Tourist Board — EMBRATUR, SCN Quadra 02, Bloco "G", Brasilia — DF-CEP 70.710-500, *Brazil*; tel +55-61 328 9100; fax +55-61 328 3517; e-mail webm@embratur.gov.br; *www.embratur.gov.br*

Cámara Argentina de Turismo, Tucamán 1610 Piso 5, Buenos Aires 1050, *Argentina*; tel +54-1 374 1699; fax +54-1 372 6902; e-mail camaratur@satlink.com

Chilean Tourism Promotion Corporation, Santa Beatriz 84-B, Providencia, Santiago, Chile; tel +56-2 235 0105; fax +56-2 235 3374

City of Reykjavik, Aoalstraetj 6, Reykjavik, Iceland; tel +354-563 2250; fax + 354-563 2249

Corfu Tourism Promotion Board, Prefecture of Corfu, 13 Samara

Street, 49 100 Corfu, *Greece*; tel +30-661 89121; fax +30-661-32525

Geneva Tourism, Route de l'Aéroport 10, CH-1215 Geneva 15, *Switzerland*; tel +41-22 909 7000; fax +41-22 909 7075; e-mail info@geneva-tourism.ch

Kansai Tourism Committee, c/o Cultural Affairs and Tourism Division, Nara Prefecture Government, 30 Noborioji-cho, Nara 630-8501, *Japan*; tel +81-742 22 1101; fax 81-742 27 7744

Lithuanian State Department of Tourism, Vilniaus 4/35, 2600 Vilnius, *Lithuania*; tel +3702-622-610; fax +3702-226-819; e-mail tb@tourism.lt; fax +3702-226-819; e-mail: tb@tourism.lt; *www.tourism.lt* or *www.travel.lt*

Nepal Depatment of Tourism, Bhrikuti Mandap, Kathmandu, *Nepal*; tel +977-1 247037/256233; fax +977-1 227281; e-mail tourism@mos.com.np; *www.south-asia.com*

Ontario Canada Tourism, 90 Bay Street, 9th Floor, Hearst Block, Toronto, Ontario M7A 2E1, *Canada*; tel +1-416-314 7367; fax +1-416-314 7504/7563

Picardy Tourist Board, 3 rue Vincent Auriol, 80011 Amiens cédex 1, *France*; tel 33-3 22 91 10 15; fax +33-3 22 97 92 96 — website *www.franceguide.com* for France nationally

Salzburg City Tourist Office, Auerspergstrasse 7, A-5020 Salzburg, *Austria*; tel +43-662 889870; fax +43-662 8898732; e-mail tourist@salzburginfo.or.at; *www.salzburginfo.or.at*

Scottish Tourist Board, 23 Ravelston Terrace, Edinburgh EH4 3EU, *Scotland*; tel 0131-332 2433; fax 0131-343 1513; *www.holiday.scotland.net*

Stockholm Information Service, Box 7542 10393, Stockholm, *Sweden*; tel +46-8 789 2400; fax +46-8 789 2450; e-mail info@stoinfo.se;www.stoinfo.se

Texas Tourism, PO Box 12728, Austin, TX 78711, *USA*; tel 512-936-0508; fax 512-936-0450; e-mail malcolms@tded.state.tx.us; *www.traveltex.com*

South Pacific Tourism Organisation — American Samoa, Cook Islands, Fiji, French Polynesia, Kiribati, New Caledonia, Niue, Papua New Guinea, Samoa, Solomon Islands, Tonga, Tuvalu and *Vanuatu* — Level 3, FNPF Place, 343-359 Victoria Parade, PO Box 13119, Suva, *Fiji Islands*; tel +679-304177; fax +679-301995; e-mail spice@is.com.fj; *www.tcsp.com*

Travel South USA — Alabama, Arkansas, Florida, Georgia, Kentucky, Mississippi, Louisiana, North Carolina, South Carolina, Tennessee, and Virginia — 3400 Peachtree Road NE, Atlanta, Georgia 30326, *USA*; tel 404-231-1790; fax 404-231-2364; e-mail tsusa@mindspring.com; *www.travel-south.com* — about going to any of these places, giving practical info

Veneto Region, Canna Regio 168, Veneto, 30121 Venice, *Italy*; tel +39-041 279 2761; fax +39-041 279 2609; e-mail sirt@saritel.it

Warsaw Tourist Office, Plac Powstanców Warszawy 2, 00-030, *Poland*; tel +48-22-8273864; fax +48-22-8263053; e-mail biuro.warsawtour@bptnet.pl; *www.Warsawtour.bptnet.pl* — you click the flag for information in English

World Tourism Organization

World Tourism Organization, and the *WTO Business Council* (Capitán Haya 42, 228020 Madrid, *Spain*; tel +34-91 567 81 00; fax +34-91 571 37 33; *www.world-tourism.org*; e-mail omt@world-tourism.org or pub@world-tourism.org) publishes international tourism studies: for example their Yearbook of *Tourism Statistics* or *World Tourism Directory* — *"an address bookfortheentiretourismindustry"*—as well as books for tourism professionals and research.

One recent *WTO Business Council* report found that *"reductions in the working week slowed considerably in the 1990s"* — contrary to the popular belief that leisure time is growing. *"As a result, working time has become more flexible, and employment and pension arrangements less secure."* This study, which surveyed leisure time in 18 countries, found very few governments were considering reductions in the length of the working week.

"For many employees, working hours have actually increased because companies are facing ever more intense global competition"

Personal Experiences

Appendix 3

A short-term job abroad

The health worker

Jennifer Coyne spent a year away, aboard the *"world's only international flying hospital."* Jennifer had been working as a senior staff nurse before she joined *ORBIS*, a non-profit organization dedicated to saving sight, in their goal to eliminate unnecessary blindness worldwide.

She says: *"I decided to join ORBIS because I could travel extensively without giving my nursing career a break. I had never been far afield and the project held a sense of adventure. I had no preconceptions about what I was getting myself into and decided to go with an open mind."*

Varna in *Bulgaria* was her first port of call. The plane — a DC-10 jet converted to medical use — targets countries in greatest need of opthalmic health; and took her to nine more destinations, including *Jordan*, *Mongolia*, *Syria*, *China*, *Cuba* and *Jamaica*. Jennifer's main concern was the exchange of knowledge and skills, which local nurses will continue to use and pass on to their peers.

In hospitals, *"management didn't listen to their nurses and were often more receptive to an outsider's advice than to act on feedback from their own nurses."* The charity also has a presence in hospitals on the ground, giving advice and saving sight.

The most difficult times for Jennifer were the screening days, where a maximum of 20 patients were selected from up to 300 every week.

"Many travel for miles, and even days in the expectations of being helped by the plane."

If you would like to make a contribution of any kind, contact ORBIS on 0207-278 5528 in the UK. For a "tour around the plane" visit www.orbis.org

The designer

Sarah Thomson went to *Bolivia* nine years ago, where she shared an apartment with her two colleagues working for an import-export company. This was bringing local handicrafts to a chain of shops in Britain. Then she travelled around and visited *Colombia, Chile* and the Andes.

She became fascinated with the way people recycled things, she says, which led her to set up her own shop in North London, and a small design company *"not just importing things but using the same ideas, and making things with everyday household objects, anything which people just have lying around."*

Hers was an unusual idea for a business; but the inspiration definitely came from abroad. *"Living out there was definitely the inspiration, the job I was doing there, and seeing how people rescue almost any object and use it again. I like adapting to new circumstances, and materials I find can be used in many ways too."*

This was an example of *"an idea I can bring home."* She still visits Bolivia — when she can — to buy goods in local markets, especially locally produced furniture, and to travel. She says enjoys her *"international lifestyle,"* which is based at home, but she travels abroad for business too, and has *"many friends all over the world."*

Medium-term work abroad

The builders

In 1998, Mark Orchard, who owns a building company in western *England,* went on vacation to *Kenya,* a 'typical' holiday resort but one where he found something very different from the usual run of tourists. He became friendly with a hotel worker he met, who invited him to see his village — which is where his story started.

Mark saw the local school, and the inadequate facilities; and when he went back home asked his colleagues in his small building firm if they could help.

They could, and did. When they went out to the village they took tools, and plenty of enthusiasm, and in just three weeks had built a new school building — to the amazement of the locals. Who had their own way of honouring their contribution to the village.

They were made — Mark, and his colleagues from the building firm—tribal elders.

Mark himself was made the chief of the Giriama tribe, *"with the power to vote on tribal issues — and I'm to be accorded all the respect due an elder of the tribe,"* he told the intrepid *Guardian* journalist who interviewed him there.

Unlikely, but true. Mark is now known by his honorific Swahili name, Ngumbad — "the hero" — and his colleagues Reg, Andy, Chris and Dave are now respectively Tswekadzonago ("wise elder"); Kadenge ("the quick one"); Chadi ("the one of many works"); and Nguma ("the smiler").

Journalism

Abroad is where my own writing career started. I was working in *France* as an English teacher when I wrote an article for a locally produced publication for English-language students. Raising my sights slightly higher, and armed only with a typewriter — in the days before PCs — I began scanning the pages of the French press — mainly *Le Monde* and *Libération* — for what I considered to be "good ideas" for stories. These, I reckoned, I could sell or somehow get to the attention of the English-language press.

Some were were ideas for stories, or interviews which I could write up later. There are many ways of producing an article — or a book like this. Which made me think about what is original when it comes to journalism.

And it sometimes, somehow worked — and I managed quite a few interviews and articles which were published; and made a bit of extra money on top of my English teaching.

This taught me something about reporting from other countries, and how this is often linked to stereotypes too: in *France*, this would be food, or *franglais*, or some small-town scandal . . . *Russia* could be crime, or poverty, or drink perhaps, which are subjects the press here in the *UK* tends to concentrate on; *Japan* used to be hard work and economic success but now tends to be unemployment, or the latest fad or fashion . . . and so it goes on, the stereotypes of the ways people think about different countries.

From a practical point of view, if you are a freelance journalist, you can probably make a little money living abroad, but not a lot.

The consultants

It sounds as if consultants offer advice; but they can be in charge of major projects.

Some will work in the voluntary sector, or for international organizations, or for private-sector companies. Some will have a 'non-visible' role, to do with organization (as we enter an increasingly 'non-visible' and information-orientated world); others will be working in a more concrete domain—in engineering, on projects in construction or architecture, or in manufacturing industry.

This difference is mainly between the secondary and tertiary sectors, making things and providing services. Also, mining and agriculture are areas where consultants are needed.

And consultancy can be truly international: almost all the recent winners of a recent *Times* newspaper 'Consultant of the Year' competition were involved in international projects, from the development of a business park in *Germany* to *"setting up an efficient customs authority in* Mozambique" to the engineering work required for the new airport in *Hong Kong, China*.

Consulting is based firmly on skills and experience which you can export to the country in question — and the jobs pages of *Overseas Jobs Express* are very good for finding this kind of skilled job — the areas of engineering, quantity surveying, telecommunications, science and technology, safety and security, roads and highways, oil and gas, mines and quarries, marine, management and information technology—and so on—all featuring in its 'JOBS' section. If you work in any one of these areas, a three-month subscription — if you were thinking of working abroad — would be a good investment: *OJE*, Premier House, Shoreham Airport, West Sussex BN43 5FF, UK; tel 01273-440220/540; fax 01273-440229; e-mail editor@overseasjobs.com; ***www.overseasjobs.com.***

The 'non-visible' project' winner in *The Times* newspaper consultancy competition was Chris Mathias, who led a *ULG Consultants* team setting up what was decribed as an agricultural market information system in *Kyrgyzstan*.

Tony Abbotts was involved in a 'visible' project: the development of the Maghara drift mine in the Sinai Desert in *Egypt* — *"the only underground coalmine in the Middle East."* This covered ten years from the first feasibility study to his move there as site manager for *IMC Group Consulting* two years later.

Some typical problems Chris Mathias encountered in Kyrgyzstan were *"uncertainty of communications and the power supply."* But this local project is now being developed into a fully national one, with the help of the World Bank.

Tony Abotts *"had to make possible the mine's development*

as a self-contained community with its own power plant and water supply. The safety of the mine depended on training the local workers, which was complicated as most were illiterate and many unable to understand English." It is now *"fully operational,"* with output due to double over the next three years.

Long-term

Voluntary work

Mark Goldring is the chief executive of the charity *VSO (Voluntary Service Overseas)*. But it was not always so.

His career started as a volunteer in *Sarawak* and East *Malaysia* in 1979, and since then he has not lost his enthusiasm for international living, spending only *"five years out of 20 at home in the UK."*

He came back to work in the VSO head office as overseas director, a job that has taken him to no less than 60 countries. Now, he is *"tied to his desk in London to a far greater degree,"* but says he bring a *"clear perspective of what works on the ground and an understanding of what is needed"* after his long experience of living and working abroad.

VSO sends skilled, committed volunteers — such as doctors, farmers, teachers, lawyers and builders — to work in partnership with local people to help them build up projects. *"The idea is to pass on experience and knowledge, to allow local people to take over the project,"* Mark says.

"People are paid according to local wage conditions, while VSO contributes to pensions and gives volunteers a small lump sum

when they return to the UK . . . We are very interested in professionals in their fifties, whose children have grown up and have, perhaps, taken early retirement, and we are starting a recruitment drive with them in mind."

Recently, the organization has been advertising for qualified primary-level teachers to act as teacher trainers.

For more information about VSO (Voluntary Service Overseas) and details of opportunities, please contact the VSO Enquiries Unit, *317 Putney Bridge Road, London SW15 2PN, UK; tel 0208-780 7500 (24 hours); e-mail enquiry@vso.org.uk; http://*www.vso.org.uk.

"Want to find out what it's really like? Chat to a returned volunteer on 0845-603 0027"

The student

Tanya Styrkas is from Moscow; and after studying first there, and then in the *UK*, she went to live in Prague, *Czech Republic* with her husband, where she has been writing her PhD thesis and looking after her young daughter.

Living there, she has found Czech people *"friendly and helpful". "The Czechs do not speak English — the older generation may speak German — so when you ask for directions it's better to have a map, so people can show you the route."*

"Now there are British shops in the centre of Prague — Marks and Spencer, Boots, Tesco — and there are several clubs for people who have just arrived, e.g. the International Women's Association of Prague *which has a hospitality meeting on Tuesdays at the President Hotel."*

Generally, this is a *"safe"* place. But *"beware of pickpockets in the city centre and on trams,"* she warns. *"Travel timetables are not so reliable; and it's better to check at stations. It's a small country, and usually going by bus is quicker than by train: the prices are similar."*

"Accommodation is very good, plentiful in the city, and especially in Vinogrady — an area where the foreign community is large."

Jobs, she says, can be found in *The Prague Post.* To work, a foreigner needs a work permit — *"which is not a problem in itself but the process is time consuming. It can be obtained in the police station for foreign workers in Prague 3."* Sometimes it is *"better to let your employer apply for a work permit on your behalf,"* she says.

Before you go, if you are coming from outside this region, Tanya recommends you take an adapter, which can be purchased at airports or on ferries *en route.* Life is *"cheaper than living in the UK, especially for travel by train and bus; and museums, the cinema, theatre, and the opera are all very affordable. But clothes are similarly expensive."*

At home abroad

Steve Cherrington and his wife Bella moved six years ago from their two-bedroom London flat to a small farmhouse near Bourges in France. *"The city had been my life. I worked for a PR company specializing in art, and my evenings were devoted to socializing, going out, dinner parties and social events."*

"With two young children, we felt it was time to make a change. But I had no experience of muddy fields or anything about the

country before we decided to move."

Bella and Steve have become . . . farmers. She had lived on a farm as a child; and Steve has a French mother, *"which led us to consider this part of the world. We felt that France was the only place we could do it; and we liked the education system and were worried about the English one."* Their eldest son is six and has just started primary school.

"He is already chattering with his schoolmates — although the change from a more laid-back style of teaching might be a bit of a shock."

Steve gave up his job. Bella — who writes about gardening, as well as looking after the garden and helping him on the small-holding — felt she could cope with the salary drop and continue her writing anywhere, with modems and fax machines, even hundreds of miles from London.

They bought the farmhouse and its five hectares of land for *"what we got for our flat."* Although the farming can't provide a full-time income, it's *"for the way of life here and to make a new start that we came."*

Some tips she offers for coping with a lower income include: *"adjusting your expectations — so you really don't need as many things as you thought —and also asking yourself what you want most out of life. And do a pros and cons list. It can crystallize your feelings."*

The traveller

On 12th March 1992, John Todd touched down at *Midway*, an island in the Pacific Ocean half way between *Japan* and *Hawaii*, and become the world's most travelled man — the first person to visit every country in the world.

"It was not like plane-spotting, or collecting," he says. *"I had already visited more than 200 countries as a student, and then as a travel agent, and it was just a question of carrying on."*

He was born in Northern Ireland; and his strong Christian beliefs have also accompanied him on his travels. At the height of the hippy era he lived in California; and he has been to no less than 379 countries, or *"territories,"* he says.

The UN only has 200 or so members, so the list is very complete: *"There are countries which are not members of the UN, like* Taiwan *and* Switzerland,*"* he says, *"and once the definition is broadened to one of sovereignty, smaller states such as* Andorra, Monaco, San Marino, *and* Luxembourg *join the number."*

And to some which didn't even used to exist. During the period covered by his travels — from his first visit to southern *Ireland* as a small boy, to this last landfall at Midway Island — *"there have been two* Germanies, *two* Koreas, *two* Vietnams, *two* Cypruses, *and two* Yemens . . .*"* He points out that the former USSR became *"at least fifteen"* countries in 1991, and *"probably contains upwards of fifty."*

"But anyone who'd been to Latvia, Ukraine *or* Uzbekistan *knew they were countries all along."*

'Race for the World' *by John Todd is published by Hodder and Stoughton, 338 Euston Road, London NW1 3BH, UK; tel 0207-873 6000; fax 0207-873 6024.*

A marriage

Eyes can meet across a crowded room; others take time to know each other; but getting married is one way many people end up living abroad and having a more international life.

Even when two people speak the same language, it isn't easy. Strong cultural divides can challenge the most stable relationship — and when a marriage is international, questions like where to live, what language to speak, and how to communicate with the in-laws can pose a problem. (Extract from the Valentine's Day issue of the 'Style' section of the *Budapest Sun*, 1122 Búdapest, Városmajor utca 13, Hungary; fax 214-0388; *www.budapestsun.com*; story by Anita Altman).

Zsuzsa Rózsa says she never thought she'd go out with a foreigner. *"I didn't want to date men who think Hungarian women aren't meant for something serious,"* she says. But when she met fiancé Robert she liked his style. *"He always planned fun activities; and he cooked for himself."*

"Hungarian guys think washing and cooking are female things, and career development is a male thing." But Robert — and Zsuzsa — had different ideas. They met through a colleague in the bank where she worked — Robert was working for a Canadian company in *Hungary* at the time — and they became friends.

Language was a problem. *"I wanted to express deep thoughts and my philosophy of life,"* she says, but, good as her English was, she found she couldn't say things clearly.

"I explained, but it wasn't easy. Rob was very patient with me." Her father wasn't bowled over by the match. *"He's a little sad I won't go hunting with him,"* says Rob. *"They could tell I*

was a nice guy and treat her well, but that's not what they envisioned for their daughter. Our communication is mostly non-verbal."

Two views of Japan

Scott Maitland was an oriental carpet restorer before he went to Japan. He got a job by *"placing ads in the English newspapers, then opened his own school, teaching from home."*

"If you are your own boss, it's simple," he says; *"but if you work at a school with a Japanese owner it can be quite difficult."* Questions of *"morality," "positions in the pecking order," "cultural difference,"* and *"adaptibility"* may all come up. Japanese people, he says, are *"both gregarious and shy. A foreigner will not be quite so constrained by social custom and will be able to move quite freely and forgiven for most trespasses."*

Xiaolin Pan is from China. She came in 1993 to look for a job before graduation; working there now as a clerk — and in an environment she finds *"short of activity."*

"There is discrimination against foreign people, of sex, or rank, of office . . . One man's management consciousness is very strong in my company," she says. *"Japanese business people refuse to make fast decisions; and even when the person is in charge, he or she won't give a definite 'yes' or 'no'."*

For herself, Xiaolin Pan says *"it is not easy"* — although good points are *"a convenient life"* like *"traffic information, shopping, good service;"* and she enjoys mixing with people and travel, recommending Nara, Kyoto and Kobe as places to visit. Getting around is easy; but *"accommodation is not good; and houses sometimes rented to foreigners without guarantee."*

And there is the difficulty of 'key money:' the deposit needed to rent a house or apartment. *"Be prepared to fork out rent plus key money in the beginning,"* Scott says. *"Key money is about ten times the monthly rent, ¥800,000 and upwards."* Apparently, there is something called 'thank you' money too.

Xiaolin says the cost of living is higher than at home; and has *"no money-saving tips."* Then there is the *"discrimination against some foreign people"* she mentions. Scott also has a deeper worry about the country — *"a good place to live if you are satisfied with materialism and comfort. Unfortunately, it seems to be completetly lacking in spirit, in vision, in a future."*

"Although this is the 'land of the gods' there is no faith here. There are business gods, entrance examination gods . . . but something fundamental seems to be missing." The plus points are *"a million things to do"* — and *"there will always be someone kind enough to help when you need it if you travel around."* But *"bring lots of money. Doing this country on the cheap is almost impossible"* — a warning echoed by many travellers to Japan.

Of his students, he says they are *"intelligent and interesting;"* accommodation is *"reasonable;"* food is *"good;"* the streets are *"safeandclean;"* the *"climate temperate . . . all in all a good place."*

How would it be if you went and lived there, and got a job in Japan? Xiaolin's advice is: *"when in Rome, do as the Romans do."*

Scott says *"it depends on the individual. I just went. Things tend to fall into place."*

*   *   *   *   *

Wake up, World! *follows a day in the life of some children around the world, on the* Oxfam educational *website:* www.oxfam.org.uk/coolplanet

If you would like to send in your own experience of living and working abroad — wherever you come from in the world — for a shorter or longer time — and include any advice for future readers of this book — please return a copy of the *Worldwide* questionnaire at the end of Chapter 5

INDEX OF COUNTRIES

You can use this Index of Countries *to find the countries / regions / territories mentioned in the main chapters of* Living and Working Abroad

INDEX OF COUNTRIES

INDEX OF ORGANIZATIONS

This Index of Organizations *is for the main companies / organizations mentioned in* A Straightforward Guide to Living and Working Abroad.

Also see the sections Direct Contacts, Personal Experiences *and* Sources of Information.

WHO TO CONTACT

Direct Contacts — pp.167 – 183

ORGANIZATIONS

INDEX OF ORGANIZATIONS

INDEX OF ORGANIZATIONS

Websites

Amazon

www.amazon.co.uk

American Airlines

www.aa.com

Amtrak

www.amtrak.com

Avis Rent-A-Car

www.avis.com

BC Rail (Canada)

www.bcrail.com

Bradman's

www.bradmans.com

Britrail

www.britrail.co.uk

Budget Rent A Car

www.budgetrentacar.com

Corona Worldwide

www.commercepark.co.uk/coronaww

easyJet

www.easyjet.com

Export Courier

www .exportcourier.co.uk

Rail Europe

www.raileurope.com

Eurolines

www.eurolines.com

Greyhound Lines

www.greyhound.com

Hertz

www.hertz.com

Hilton Hotels

www.hilton.com

Holiday Inn

www.holiday-inn.com

Lufthansa

www.lufthansa.co.uk

Marriott International

www.marriott.com

Overseas Jobs Express

www.overseasjobs.com

Sillabo

www.sillabo.com

TNT Magazine

www.tntmagco.uk

VSO

www.vso.org.uk

Weather–24-hour Forecast

www.weather.netscape.com

World Travel Guide

www.wtgonline.com

YHA Adventure Shops

www.yhaadventure.co.uk

www.**jobprofiles**.com/

agrZookeeper2.htmzzz